- THE NEW -
PRESSURE
-COOKER-
COOKBOOK

· THE NEW ·
PRESSURE
·COOKER·
COOKBOOK

A complete guide to
meals in minutes
using today's stress-free
pressure cooker

· PAT DAILEY ·

CB

CONTEMPORARY
BOOKS

CHICAGO

Library of Congress Cataloging-in-Publication Data

Dailey, Pat.
    The new pressure cooker cookbook / Pat Dailey.
        p.   cm.
    ISBN 0-8092-4186-2
    1. Pressure cookery.   I. Title.
TX840.P7D35   1990
641.5'87—dc20   89-71207
                                                         CIP

Published by Contemporary Books, Inc.
Two Prudential Plaza, Chicago, Illinois 60601-6790
Manufactured in the United States of America
International Standard Book Number: 0-8092-4186-2

CONTENTS

ACKNOWLEDGMENTS

Few things in life are done as a solo venture. Even though it was I who dreamed up the recipes, tested them, retested them, and cleaned up an endless stream of dishes, I was not without a wonderful support system. To the many people who coached and encouraged, tasted, suggested, commented, and thought of every possible pressure cooker pun, I'll resort to an old truism: I couldn't have done it without you. I hope that when I was deep in the midst (and mists) of the project, my gratitude was apparent. Now, with the work behind me, let me extend the most genuine and heartfelt thanks.

Special thanks go to Pat Tennison, whose role in all of this was greatly appreciated.

The makers of pressure cookers were generous and forthcoming in their support and assistance. I'd especially like to thank the folks at Lentrade, Cuisinarts, Kuhn-Rikon, Mirro, Presto, T-Fal, and Coranco.

And finally, Linda Gray, editor extraordinaire, gets a round of applause for making it all seem so easy. Though I never took her up on it, I was quite touched by her offer to help me do my grocery shopping. That seems to be going above and beyond the call of what an editor is expected to do.

1
INTRODUCTION

There are, I'm convinced, two types of people in the world—those who don't have a pressure cooker and those who can't live without theirs. It seems like one of those irrefutable quirks of nature that you can't have a pressure cooker and not think it's the greatest thing in the kitchen. When I start talking about pressure cookers, which I'm wont to do on occasion, people who have a pressure cooker practically trip over their words in excitement. Simply put, they can't say enough about it. "I can't imagine why everyone on earth doesn't have one" and "It's the greatest thing I've ever seen" are typical testimonials. Those who don't have a pressure cooker (at least not yet, anyway, though they're bound to catch on pretty soon) prefer to tell archaic stories about why they don't have one. But more on that later.

My own enthusiasm for the pressure cooker began several years ago, and all it took was an instant. One of the sleek and shiny new models was being demonstrated as I happened by. My first inclination, thanks to all the stories I'd heard about those ill-behaved pressure cookers, was to turn and run. After all, conventional wisdom had it that these things were positively explosive, and frankly I didn't want to be in the line of fire when the lamb shanks became airborne projectiles. But curiosity overcame any trepidations I had, so I stayed and watched the pressure cooker do all sorts of marvelous things—quickly and without blowing its cover.

Speed is only half of the package, though. What really drew me

1

into the fold was that the food tasted good—make that great. It didn't taste like fast food, or something that had cooked in minutes when it was meant to take hours. It was instant, wonderful, lick-my-fingers gratification. I knew I was hooked.

That the pressure cooker and I clicked so well isn't too surprising given my tendencies in the kitchen. The aphorism that a watched pot never boils never had a great effect on me. If there is food on the stove, chances are I'm hovering about, opening the pot, stirring, checking, tasting, and just generally being overly attentive. And therein lies the real beauty of the pressure cooker. Because it's not designed to be opened easily, I don't feel compelled to stand guard and take periodic peeks. With my trusty timer on a rope, I can actually leave the kitchen. Even if I do hang around the stove, my designated term is much shorter because foods cook so much more quickly in the pressure cooker.

In addition to the speedy nature of pressure cookers, several other advantages of these marvels are worth noting. First, pressure cookers are very energy efficient. Once they've got a full head of steam going, the stove can be turned down to a mere whisper. This accomplishes two things—it saves money and it keeps the kitchen cool, something that will be enormously appreciated in the summer.

Pressure cookers can be a budgetary ally on another front. For example, many of the less expensive cuts of meat are lauded for their marvelous flavor and, ultimately, their fall-apart tenderness. But this much-heralded taste comes about only after cooking—lots of cooking. Thus, in spite of their lower cost, these meats extract much from the cook in terms of time and energy. Unless, of course, the pressure cooker is used. Then low-cost meats become truly practical to use on a day-to-day basis.

And certainly not to be overlooked in these health-conscious times is how prudent the use of a pressure cooker can be when it comes to healthwise cooking. Two traits stand out. First, all foods can be cooked in the pressure cooker without any added fat or oil. While some of the recipes I have created for this book use butter or oil to brown meat, this step, and hence the fat, can always be omitted by those looking to reduce their intake of fat. Second, because foods cook quickly and in a tightly closed chamber, very few nutrients are lost.

Comparisons between the microwave oven and the pressure cooker are inevitable, although not necessarily logical. Yes, both do cook foods more quickly. And yes, they're both wonderful. But it's a classic apples-and-oranges situation. Both are excellent for what they do. And what one does, the other doesn't always do as well. But that's OK. In an ideal situation, a kitchen has both. A pressure cooker is great for cooking many meats, soups, stews, beans, and rice. Microwave ovens reheat foods, do a terrific job of making popcorn, cooking fish and vegetables, and so on. So resist the temptation to say that one is better than the other. Both have their merits and both have a place in the kitchen.

Somewhere in the back of your mind, you just might be asking why, if pressure cookers are so great, did they all but disappear from American kitchens during the 1960s. Times changed. Cooks were tantalized by all the convenience foods that inundated the supermarkets and by the wonderful sense of freedom such foods offered. For many, cooking became a matter of opening cans, heating frozen dinners, and making Jell-O molds. For the time being, pressure cookers were shoved to the back burner, making room for TV dinners and microwave ovens. Then, when cooking got serious again, nouvelle cuisine stormed the country, and somehow nouvelle and pressure cookers didn't jibe. Baby vegetables with beurre blanc were most unlikely candidates for the pressure cooker.

Once again, though, the times and tides are turning. People need the convenience of quick cooking, but they don't always want foods that taste as though they were cooked quickly. The complex flavors of a long-simmered stew, the fall-off-the-bone tenderness of a veal shank, the cozy comfort of a big kettle of soup, all haunt us now and then. And with the pressure cooker, such dishes are, happily, quite within the reach of almost any cook, even the most time-pressed.

2
THE PRESSURE PRINCIPLE: UNDERSTANDING AND WORKING WITH YOUR PRESSURE COOKER

■

Just what is it about pressure cookers that makes them turn rock-hard rutabaga into a tender puree in minutes, a recalcitrant roast into a fork-tender treat in less than an hour? Attribute these transformations to the pressure principle, the culinary miracles of steam, and a bit of scientific alchemy. Although it certainly isn't necessary to know all the little nuts and bolts of why a pressure cooker cooks faster, it's nice to have some scientific insight into this seemingly magical cooking process.

There are no mysterious waves, no radiation, just good old heat and water at work in a pressure cooker. Water put over heat boils and then creates steam. Look at the cover of a pressure cooker and you'll see that inside, along the inside of the rim, is a rubber sealing ring or gasket. This ensures that once the pressure cooker is properly closed and locked, nothing can escape—not even so much as an ephemeral cloud of steam. In this tightly sealed environment, the steam, which has no place to escape to, builds up inside the cooker and creates pressure. With the increased pressure bearing down on the surface of the liquid, the water molecules don't break up to create steam as readily and thus produce more heat. In doing so, the boiling point of water is raised from 212° F (at sea level) to 250° F when 15 pounds of pressure have built up inside the cooker.

Then, as if the superheated atmosphere weren't enough, the forces of pressure go to work at breaking down and softening fibrous parts. This double-fisted assault on the food conspires to cook it in anywhere from one third to one tenth the original time.

Pressure cookers still have a bit of an explosive reputation lingering from their past, which needs to be erased once and for all. There is a litany of stories, all with a common theme, that people who don't have a pressure cooker love to tell. Everyone has heard the tale of the pressure cooker that caused a nuclear meltdown or the soup that ate the kitchen. Even I have my own story. As a child, I was alternately fascinated and terrorized by the story my mother told of watching a pressure cooker explode right before her very eyes. A friend tells of the chop suey that literally flew from pressure cooker to ceiling, leaving peeled, chipping paint in its wake. And so on.

While such accidents were possible in the old generation of pressure cookers, usually at the hands of a careless cook, there's nary a chance of them happening in the new models. In a belt-and-suspenders system of safety, modern pressure cookers have a safety valve that releases excess steam should the cook forget to turn down the heat when the pressure reaches the proper level. And locking mechanisms are designed so they can't be opened until every last pouf of steam has been safely released.

Most manufacturers voluntarily submit their pressure cookers to the rigors of testing by Underwriters Laboratories. At UL, they do everything you're not supposed to do to a pressure cooker, all in the hopes of finding its flaws. They override the safety valves, build up 100 pounds of pressure inside the cooker, and generally abuse it, but happily to no avail. Still no popped tops.

Other drawbacks that sent pressure cookers into temporary hiding in the 1960s and '70s have also been eliminated. The new generation of pressure cookers combines all the surefire safety assurances with foolproof, user-friendly features. Hissing and steaming, clacking and "eruptability" are all behind them now, and to that I say *amen*. Manufacturers have introduced sleek new models that combine high-tech wizardry with good old-fashioned appeal.

Like other pots and pans, pressure cookers come in a wide range of sizes. Most companies make 4-, 6-, 8-, and sometimes 10-quart cookers. There are smaller ones as well. One Swiss company makes a handy 2-liter (about 2 quarts) pressure fryer that looks like a chicken fryer. For singles or couples, it's a convenient size and has the added advantage of browning foods very well. Although it is called a pressure fryer, it is not to be confused with the pressure deep-fat fryers that were sold a decade or so ago. Pressure cookers are not designed for deep-fat frying.

All of the recipes in this book were tested in a 6-quart pressure cooker. Although there are smaller and larger ones on the market, the vast majority of pressure cookers sold are 6-quart, and with good reason. A six-quart cooker is a good, practical size for most families. Before you protest that 6 quarts sounds like a big pot, understand that you don't fill a 6-quart pressure cooker with 6 quarts of food, only 4 quarts. And you can, of course, fill it with much less.

If you have a smaller pressure cooker, check your instruction manual to make sure that the recipe doesn't exceed the recommended limit of your cooker. Many of these recipes will fit, but do make sure before proceeding. Cut them down to size as necessary. And if you aren't certain, just be sure never to fill the pressure cooker more than two-thirds full. Many of them have little indicator lines showing the maximum fill line.

Although it seems to be stating the obvious, the best advice I can give is to read through your instruction book before you even step into the kitchen with your new pressure cooker. This means the whole book, not just the section that tells you how to put the cover on. Once you learn how to assemble the pressure cooker, it is awfully tempting to move on to a recipe. Take the extra time to learn about your new pressure cooker. Every page in the instruction book contains little snippets of information that may help you and will allow for trouble-free operation. For instance, you'll find out what the capacity of your pressure cooker really is. You'll learn when and how to clean the steam-vent assembly. You'll learn how much liquid to add. Some pressure cooker parts are dishwasher safe, while others may not be. And so on. So read the book.

After reading the instruction book, you'll also be conversant with the language of pressure cookers. Fortunately, there is not a huge battery of parts and accessories to become familiar with, and the lingo will come easily. In addition to the pressure cooker itself, which consists of a kettle and a cover, as well as a rubber sealing ring that fits inside the rim of the cover, most units come with a trivet or cooking rack. Increasingly, more of them also come with a removable steamer basket, which is a wonderful and, to my mind, indispensable adjunct to the pressure cooker. If a steamer basket was not included with your pressure cooker, see if one can be ordered from the manufacturer or find one that easily fits inside your cooker.

I tend to err on the side of caution, which isn't the worst way to be. Such a philosophy prompts me to suggest that if you inherited your grandmother's dearly beloved pressure cooker, you should trade it in for a new one. The new safety features are quite reassuring. While the chances I'll need them are next to nothing, they make so much sense that I can't envisage not taking advantage of them. And while it's true that most of the mishaps were the result of a cook's not following pressure cooker protocol, the newer models leave less of a margin for error. And, as you ponder how nice and clean your kitchen ceiling is, it's nice to know that your pressure cooker will never be the cause of your having to scrape spaghetti sauce off of it.

Cooking Times

A word on the timing. Each recipe has two or three lines that indicate roughly how long it will take to make it, from getting started with cutting and chopping right through to the finish. The preparation time isn't meant to be a race against the clock. Consider it a guideline. If it takes a little less or a little more time, then so be it. No one is timing you, so relax. Some of the recipes also call for marinating or standing time. Four hours is usually adequate for flavors to mix and mingle. If you can leave the dish longer, do so. It will only get better. The advance work can be done the night before or even the morning of the day it is to be served.

The cooking times given are usually for the cooking that begins once the food is in the pressure cooker. *The pressure cooking time begins when the specified level of pressure is reached, not when the cooker is put over a flame.* Though it may seem a little misleading not to include the time it takes for full pressure to be reached, there is a more precise baseline, calculated from the moment full pressure is reached. The time it takes for the food to reach full pressure will always vary depending on how much food is in the pressure cooker, the temperature and density of it, how hot the stove gets, the size of the pressure cooker, the amount of liquid, and so on.

It never takes long for the pressure to come up, though—just a matter of a few short minutes. Always use high heat to bring the pressure up. Also, for soups and the like, you might want to put the liquid in the pressure cooker and start heating it while you prepare the rest of the ingredients. This gives you a head start on the cooking time.

It's a good idea to keep a close eye on the pressure indicator as it is coming up to pressure so you can start timing when pressure is reached. Then, once you've adjusted the heat to a lower level, you can set the timer (and yes, a timer is very highly recommended as a companion piece to the pressure cooker) and go on about your business. The pressure cooker will ask for no further attention. If you happen to hear it hissing, it's only telling you that the heat is too high, not that anything untoward is happening inside the cooker. Turn the heat down a bit more but not so much that the pressure drops below the suggested cooking level.

Other cooking time involves either sautéing or browning, or the reducing of a sauce after the food has been cooked. One recipe is finished on the barbecue grill. This additional cooking time is usually minimal.

Letting Off the Steam

When the cooking is complete, there are several ways the pressure can be released. The first is to let steam dissipate by itself, inside the sealed cooker (sealed because the lid won't come off until every last bit of pressure has safely dissipated). Depending on a variety of factors, this can take anywhere from 2 or 3 minutes to as long as 20 minutes. Some recipes in this book recommend that the pressure be allowed to subside naturally, either so the food can benefit from further cooking that goes on at this time or so that any frothing that may be going on inside the pot will settle down before the lid is removed. It's also worth pointing out that if the cover is left in place, the food will stay hot for quite a long time, meaning that dinner can wait a few minutes without getting cold.

Many pressure cookers have a locking mechanism that can be disengaged to let steam escape. Although this lets a pouf of steam escape into the kitchen, the steam is not so hot that it warms the kitchen. When using the locking mechanism, always be sure to direct the steam away from you.

And, finally, all pressure cookers can be transferred from the stove to the sink, where a stream of cold water pouring over the lid will quickly bring the pressure down. Although this sounds like a clumsy task, it really isn't at all and in fact has become the method of choice for me. It's quick, it's silent, and it doesn't let steam escape into the kitchen. One suggestion—always use a pot holder when transferring the cooker to the sink. The handles usually don't get so hot that they can't be handled, but I find that, under the weight of the cooker and its contents, many of the handles are uncomfortable to hold. A pot holder acts as a cushion.

When the pressure is allowed to drop of its own accord, there's a good chance that the cooker will develop a vapor lock, making it impossible to open the cover without first returning the cooker very briefly to the stove. If your pressure cooker won't open, never try to force it. First, make sure all the pressure has been released. If it has and the lid still won't budge, a vapor lock is probably the culprit. Put the cooker over a medium flame for up to a minute until the cover loosens.

This seems like a good place to inject a word of caution. The food inside a pressure cooker is indeed hot. Even after the cover is removed, it can be hotter than anything you have ever cooked in an open pan. So when you get out that tasting spoon, be forewarned that it's pretty hot stuff in there. Let the food cool sufficiently before diving in.

When you start cooking with the pressure cooker, understand that it takes some getting used to. It's not at all unlike making crepes or pressed cookies. The first ones, though edible, never turn out quite right, but subsequent batches are masterful and leave you feeling quite accomplished. And so it is with food prepared in the pressure cooker.

All of this said, it's time to get to the heart of the matter—84 recipes designed to flaunt the marvelous abilities of the pressure cooker. Enjoy!

3
SOUPS

∎

FRESH CREAM OF TOMATO SOUP

CREAM OF CURRIED EGGPLANT SOUP

CREOLE CREAM OF ONION SOUP

FARMERS' MARKET VEGETABLE CHOWDER

FENNEL AND SCALLOP BISQUE

GOLDEN HARVEST ROOT SOUP

WILD RICE AND MUSHROOM SOUP

LENTIL SOUP

BEEF, BARLEY, AND VEGETABLE SOUP

HOPPIN' JOHN SOUP

CAPITOL BEAN SOUP

CHICKEN STOCK

BEEF STOCK

As fate—and luck—would have it, the very first thing I ever made in a pressure cooker was soup. Had I been tempted to make something more fussy and demanding, I might not have been as quick to realize the enormous charms of this newcomer to my kitchen. But as it was, the soup was a breeze to make, and it was love at first bite. Now, every time I make soup in the pressure

11

cooker, I can't help but think it is absolutely the most sensible, timewise way of doing it. Why, I wonder, would anyone opt for other methods of cooking that take three or four times as long? So far, I haven't come up with one plausible reason.

Near-record speed is only one trait worth mentioning. Soups emerge from the pressure cooker with rich, robust flavors, the kind that taste as though they took hours to develop. Purees are positively silken. Colors remain lively and vibrant. Each and every vegetable retains its identity and character. Need I say more?

Happily, almost any soup recipe can be adapted to the pressure cooker. There are several things to keep in mind when doing so. First, there will be practically no evaporation, so you might want to cut back slightly on the liquid, especially if the original recipe calls for simmering the soup without a cover. Also, most vegetables cook fairly quickly. If they are combined with ingredients such as beans, rice, or ham hocks that take longer to cook, add the vegetables toward the end of the cooking so they don't get too mushy. Even the hardest vegetables like rutabaga and beets will be soft after cooking for 15 minutes, especially if they are cut into thin slices. Softer varieties take even less time.

A word of warning: Most pressure cooker manufacturers as well as the U.S.A. Dry Pea and Lentil Industry don't recommend cooking split pea soup in the pressure cooker. They cite excessive foaming as a problem. Also, the skins can conceivably clog the steam vent. With this in mind, you might want to cook pea soup the time-honored way—in a conventional pot.

This chapter is rounded out with recipes for homemade stocks. For the small amount of effort they require, they pay handsomely with big dividends. While canned stocks and broths are indeed a godsend, they don't begin to match a homemade stock when it comes to richness of flavor. And, with homemade, you can easily control the amount of salt in the stock. Homemade stocks can be very economical as well, often costing next to nothing to prepare. I keep a bag of chicken backs, necks, and bones in the freezer, adding to it each time I cut up a chicken or bone some breasts. In no time, I have the right collection of bones to fill up a pot. Some butchers can be talked out of beef bones for stock. Even if purchased, they're pretty inexpensive. Then, all the stock takes is a few vegetables, most of which may be in the larder anyway.

FRESH CREAM OF TOMATO SOUP

Fresh tomato soup is one of the great glories of summer but, alas, of summer only. It is only worth making when the tomatoes are picture-perfect specimens—red, ripe, lush, and bursting with sunny flavor. No other liquid is added to the soup made in the pressure cooker, so the taste is mainly that of the tomatoes, a wonderful sensation if there ever was one. The cream is a divine indulgence. Without it, the soup is rosier and less rich, but still irresistible.

Preparation time: 10 minutes
Pressure cooking time: 15 minutes
Other cooking time: 5 minutes

Yield: About 5 cups

1 small clove garlic
3 medium leeks, white part only
1 tablespoon unsalted butter
3 pounds vine-ripened, summer tomatoes
2 to 3 tablespoons light brown sugar
1 cup whipping cream, if desired
Small pinch ground allspice
Salt and freshly ground black pepper to taste

1.   Mince the garlic. Cut the leeks into thin slices. Melt the butter in the pressure cooker. Add the leeks and garlic and cook over medium heat until the leeks are wilted, about 4 minutes.

2.   Core the tomatoes and chop coarse. Add to the pan along with 2 tablespoons brown sugar. Cover pressure cooker and bring up to full pressure (15 pounds). Reduce heat to stabilize pressure and cook for 15 minutes. Release pressure.

3.   Strain the solids from the liquid, reserving both. Puree the solids in a blender, then press through a fine strainer to remove the tomato skin and seeds. Reserve 1 cup of the cooking liquid and stir the strained puree back into the remaining cooking liquid. Add the cream, if desired, the allspice, and salt and pepper to taste. Taste, then add the remaining 1 tablespoon brown sugar if the soup is too acidic. Add the additional cooking liquid if the soup is too thick. The soup can be served hot or chilled. Adjust the seasoning at serving time.

CREAM OF CURRIED EGGPLANT SOUP

Fresh herbs and curry powder give eggplant a hauntingly delicious flavor. This silky-smooth soup, the same tawny gold hue as curry powder, can be served warm or chilled.

Preparation time: 10 minutes
Pressure cooking time: 10 minutes
Other cooking time: 7 minutes

Yield: 4 cups

1 medium eggplant, about 12 ounces
1 large sweet onion, about 10 ounces
1 medium potato, about 6 ounces
2 medium stalks celery
3 tablespoons unsalted butter
2½ teaspoons curry powder
¼ teaspoon ground coriander
2½ cups chicken stock or broth
½ cup fresh basil leaves
¼ cup fresh cilantro leaves
¼ cup whipping cream
Salt and freshly ground black pepper to taste

1.   Peel the eggplant, onion, and potato and cut into thin slices. Remove the strings from the celery with a vegetable peeler and slice the celery.

2.   Melt the butter in the pressure cooker. Add eggplant, onion, potato, and celery. Cook over medium heat, stirring occasionally, until onions are soft, about 5 minutes. Add curry powder and coriander and cook 1 minute.

3.   Add chicken stock or broth, cover pressure cooker, and bring up to full pressure (15 pounds). Reduce heat to stabilize pressure and cook 10 minutes. Release pressure. Strain solids from liquid, reserving both.

4.   Puree solids, basil, and cilantro in blender or food processor. Combine with the reserved cooking liquid and add the cream and salt and pepper to taste. Serve hot or chilled.

CREOLE CREAM OF ONION SOUP

Smooth and creamy white, this soup surprises with a mildly spicy kick from the andouille sausage and cayenne pepper.

Several types of super-sweet onions are in the market from spring through summer. Try to use Vidalias, Mauis, Texas 1040s, or Walla Wallas if possible. When they're not in season, select sweet Bermuda onions for the best flavor.

Preparation time: 10 minutes
Pressure cooking time: 10 minutes
Other cooking time: 10 minutes

Yield: 4 cups

5 ounces andouille sausage
1½ pounds sweet onions
1 small potato, about 4 ounces, peeled
1 large clove garlic
2 tablespoons dry sherry
½ teaspoon dried thyme
⅛ to ¼ teaspoon cayenne pepper
1 bay leaf
2 cups chicken stock or broth
½ cup half-and-half or whipping cream

1.   Cut the sausage into ¼-inch-thick slices, then dice the slices. Cut the onions and potato into thin slices, either by hand or in food processor. Mince the garlic.

2.   Cook the sausage in the pressure cooker, uncovered, over medium heat until the fat is rendered, about 5 minutes. Remove the sausage with a slotted spoon and set aside. Deglaze the pan with the sherry, adding it while the pan is still hot and stirring to dissolve the browned bits from the bottom. Add the onions, potato, and garlic and cook over high heat, stirring often, until they are soft, about 5 minutes. Stir in the thyme, cayenne pepper, and bay leaf.

3.   Add the stock or broth, cover the pressure cooker, and bring up to full pressure (15 pounds). Reduce heat to stabilize pressure and cook for 10 minutes. Release pressure.

4.   Remove and discard the bay leaf. Strain the solids from the liquid, reserving both. Puree the solids in food processor or blender. Stir the puree back into the reserved cooking liquid along with the half-and-half or cream and the sausage. Reheat briefly, without letting soup come to a boil. Serve hot. The soup can be refrigerated up to 3 days.

Note: Andouille sausage is a creole-style sausage with a peppery bite, made from pork and spices. It can be found in some super-markets as well as in specialty food stores. If andouille is not available, a garlicky smoked sausage in casing can be substituted along with red pepper sauce to taste.

FARMERS' MARKET VEGETABLE CHOWDER

This creamy, colorful chowder combines many delicious vegetables and accents them with a bit of smoked ham. Improvisation is easy. Kohlrabi can be used in place of the potato, broccoli in lieu of cauliflower, and peas instead of corn.

Preparation time: 20 minutes
Pressure cooking time: 1 minute
Other cooking time: 5 minutes

Yield: About 6 cups

1 medium Idaho potato, about 10 ounces
1 medium onion, about 4 ounces
2 cups small cauliflowerets
1 cup chicken stock or broth
½ teaspoon dried thyme
3 cups milk
1½ cups diced smoked ham
1¼ cups fresh or thawed frozen corn
1 small red bell pepper, diced
⅔ cup shredded American cheese
2 tablespoons flour
¼ cup fresh minced parsley or cilantro
Salt and freshly ground black pepper to taste

1.   Peel the potato and cut into ½-inch cubes. Dice the onion. Place in pressure cooker along with cauliflowerets, stock or broth, and thyme. Cover pressure cooker and bring up to full pressure (15 pounds). Reduce heat to stabilize pressure and cook for 1 minute. Release pressure.

2.   Add 2¾ cups milk, the ham, corn, red peppers, and cheese. Stir flour into remaining ¼ cup of milk and add to pot. Cook over high heat, uncovered, until cheese is melted and soup is hot, about 5 minutes. Add parsley or cilantro and salt and pepper to taste. Serve hot.

FENNEL AND SCALLOP BISQUE

A newcomer to many markets, fennel has a delicate, light flavor
that is sure to find many new fans. Its texture suggests celery and
so do its looks. The flavor is vaguely like that of licorice but in a very
refined way. Here, fennel is paired with scallops in a creamy, pure
white soup. For formal dinners, the soup can be served as a first
course. Or make a meal of it by adding a green salad, topped with
cheese, and a loaf of bread.

Preparation time: 15 minutes
Pressure cooking time: 10 minutes
Other cooking time: 7 minutes

Yield: 4½ cups

2 small fennel bulbs, about 1¼ pounds total
1 medium onion, about 6 ounces
1 medium red potato, about 6 ounces, peeled
1 stalk celery
1 large clove garlic
3 tablespoons unsalted butter
¼ pound sea scallops
2 cups fish stock, or 1 cup clam juice and 1 cup water
¼ cup dry white wine
½ cup whipping cream
½ teaspoon salt
Freshly ground white pepper to taste
Freshly grated nutmeg to taste

1.   Trim the long stalks from the fennel down to the bulb. Peel the
outside of the bulb, remove the core, and cut the bulb into thin
slices. Cut the onion and potato into thin slices. Remove the strings
from the celery with a vegetable peeler and cut celery into thin
slices. Mince the garlic.

2.   Melt the butter in the pressure cooker. Add the fennel, onion,
potato, celery, and garlic and cook over medium-high heat, stirring
often, until soft, about 7 minutes.

3.   Rinse and drain the scallops. Add scallops, fish stock or clam juice and water, and wine to the pressure cooker. Cover and bring up to full pressure (15 pounds), then reduce heat to stabilize pressure. Cook for 10 minutes. Release pressure.

4.   Strain the solids from the liquid, reserving both. Puree the solids in blender or food processor. Stir the puree back into the liquid and add the cream and salt, and pepper and nutmeg to taste. Serve hot. The soup can be made a day in advance and refrigerated. Reheat gently, without letting soup come to a boil, and adjust seasoning before serving.

GOLDEN HARVEST ROOT SOUP

Two vitamin-rich vegetables are combined in a deliciously different soup that flaunts a warm mix of flavors. The maple gives an underlying hint of sweetness, the lemon a clean, refreshing finish. Even though the ingredients suggest autumn, the soup can be served chilled on warm Indian summer days.

Preparation time: 10 minutes
Pressure cooking time: 10 minutes

Yield: 4½ cups

1 large sweet potato, about 12 ounces
3 large carrots, about 10 ounces total
1 medium onion, about 4 ounces
2½ to 3 cups chicken stock or broth
1 tablespoon maple syrup
2 strips lemon zest, approximately 2 inches by ½ inch
¼ teaspoon ground cinnamon
½ cup half-and-half, if desired
Salt to taste

1.   Peel the sweet potato, carrots, and onion and cut them into thin slices.

2.   Combine vegetables, 2½ cups chicken stock or broth, maple syrup, lemon zest, and cinnamon in pressure cooker. Cover and bring up to full pressure (15 pounds). Reduce heat to stabilize pressure and cook for 10 minutes. Release pressure and strain the solids from the liquid, reserving both. Remove the lemon zest from the vegetables.

3.   Puree the vegetables in a blender or food processor and stir back into the liquid along with the half-and-half, if used. Add remaining ½ cup stock or broth if the soup is too thick. Season with salt to taste. Serve hot or chilled. The soup can be refrigerated for 3 days or frozen.

WILD RICE AND MUSHROOM SOUP

This is an old favorite that adapts particularly well to the pressure cooker. The rice, with its earthy, nutty taste, is favorably enhanced by the aromatic vegetables and sherry. It's substantial enough to serve as a main-dish soup for a light meal, although cooked chicken can be added at the end of cooking for a heartier offering.

Preparation time: 15 minutes
Pressure cooking time: 22 minutes
Other cooking time: 3 minutes

Yield: 5 cups

½ cup wild rice
4 cups chicken stock or broth
1 branch fresh thyme, or ¼ teaspoon dried thyme leaves
1 medium onion, about 5 ounces
2 medium stalks celery
4 small, slender carrots
2 tablespoons flour
2 tablespoons softened unsalted butter
6 ounces small mushrooms, sliced
¼ cup dry sherry
1 cup whipping cream
Freshly grated nutmeg to taste
Salt and freshly ground black pepper to taste

1.   Combine the wild rice, stock or broth, and thyme in the pressure cooker. Cover pressure cooker and bring up to full pressure (15 pounds). Reduce heat to stabilize pressure and cook for 20 minutes.

2.   While the rice is cooking, dice the onion, celery, and carrots. When the rice has cooked for 20 minutes, release pressure and add onion, celery, and carrots. Cover and bring up to full pressure (15 pounds). Reduce heat to stabilize pressure and cook for 2 minutes. Release pressure.

3.   Stir the flour into the butter to make a smooth paste. Add to the soup along with mushrooms and sherry. Cook, uncovered, just until the mushrooms soften, 2 to 3 minutes. Remove from heat and add the cream and nutmeg, and salt and pepper to taste. Soup can be made several days in advance and refrigerated.

LENTIL SOUP

Lentils are a nutritional powerhouse, full of protein and fiber, making them a best bet for healthy eating. Here, they give substance to a meal-in-a-bowl soup that is ideal for blustery days. The sausage can be left out if you prefer a meatless soup, but by no means leave out the balsamic vinegar. It lends a final fillip of freshness and flavor.

Preparation time: 10 minutes
Pressure cooking time: 15 minutes
Other cooking time: 5 minutes

Yield: 6 cups

1 large onion, about 6 ounces
2 tablespoons vegetable oil
¾ cup brown lentils
4 cups chicken stock or broth
1 14½-ounce can tomatoes, chopped, reserving liquid
1 tablespoon light brown sugar
1 bay leaf
¼ teaspoon crushed red pepper flakes
3 medium stalks celery, diced
1 medium red bell pepper, cored and diced
*8 to 12 ounces smoked garlic sausage or other sausage, cut into ¼-
    inch-thick slices*
Salt and freshly ground black pepper to taste
2 to 3 tablespoons balsamic vinegar

1.   Chop the onion. Heat the oil in the pressure cooker. Add the onion and cook over medium heat until softened, about 5 minutes.

2.   Add the lentils, stock or broth, tomatoes and their liquid, brown sugar, bay leaf, and red pepper flakes. Cover pressure cooker and bring up to full pressure (15 pounds). Reduce heat to stabilize pressure and cook for 10 minutes.

3.   Release pressure. Add the vegetables, sausage, and salt and pepper to taste. Cover pressure cooker and bring up to full pressure (15 pounds). Reduce heat to stabilize pressure and cook for 5 minutes. Release the pressure. Add vinegar to taste. Soup can be made in advance and refrigerated for up to 4 days or frozen.

BEEF, BARLEY, AND VEGETABLE SOUP

A cross between a soup and a stew, this is a perfect supper for midwinter warm-ups. Serve it with a salad or cole slaw and warm rolls with butter.

Preparation time: 15 minutes
Pressure cooking time: 20 minutes
Other cooking time: 5 minutes

Yield: 8 cups

1¼ pounds lean ground beef
1 28-ounce can crushed tomatoes
2½ cups water
½ cup barley
3 large carrots, about 8 ounces total
2 medium stalks celery
1 large Idaho potato, about 10 ounces
1 medium onion, about 6 ounces
1 small clove garlic
½ teaspoon dried basil
½ teaspoon dried thyme leaves
½ teaspoon dried rosemary
½ teaspoon dried marjoram
¾ teaspoon salt
Freshly ground black pepper to taste

1.　Brown the beef in the pressure cooker. Drain off any fat. Add the tomatoes, water, and barley. Cover pressure cooker and bring up to full pressure (15 pounds). Reduce heat to stabilize and cook for 10 minutes.

2.　While the soup is cooking, split the carrots in half lengthwise, then cut into ¼-inch-thick slices. Cut the celery into ¼-inch-thick slices. Peel and dice the potato. Dice the onion and mince the garlic.

3.　When the soup has cooked for 10 minutes, release pressure and add the vegetables, basil, thyme, rosemary, marjoram, salt, and pepper to taste. Cover pressure cooker and bring up to full pressure (15 pounds). Reduce the heat until pressure is stabilized and cook 10 minutes longer. Release the pressure. The soup can be refrigerated for up to 4 days or frozen.

HOPPIN' JOHN SOUP

Hoppin' John is a distinctively Southern dish of black-eyed peas and rice, cooked up with lots of bacon or ham. Legend has it that it brings good luck if eaten on New Year's Day. And because it is so closely aligned with that particular holiday, it has also come to be regarded as a cure for hangovers. Here, the same ingredients are simmered into an immensely satisfying soup, good enough to cure whatever ails you. The good luck is the pressure cooker. It cooks the black-eyed peas in a wink.

Bacon is used because it happens to be the most convenient of many different options. Diced country ham can be used in its place, as can tasso (a highly seasoned Cajun smoked ham) or andouille sausage, typical Louisiana ingredients.

Preparation time: 10 minutes plus soaking time
Pressure cooking time: 8 minutes
Other cooking time: 10 minutes

Yield: 5 cups

½ cup black-eyed peas
1 medium onion, about 4 ounces
2 medium stalks celery
4 to 6 slices bacon, cut into small pieces
¼ cup long grain rice
4 cups chicken stock or broth
½ teaspoon dried thyme
⅛ teaspoon cayenne pepper
Dash red pepper sauce
1 cup peeled, seeded, and diced tomatoes (use fresh or well-
*   drained canned)*
1 small jalapeño or serrano pepper, minced
½ cup minced cilantro leaves
Salt and freshly ground black pepper to taste

1.   Soak the peas as directed (see Index). Drain well.

2.   Dice the onion and celery. Brown the bacon in the pressure cooker. Remove it with a slotted spoon and set aside. Pour off all but 2 tablespoons fat from the pan. Add the onion and celery and cook over medium heat until softened, about 5 minutes.

3.   Add the soaked peas, rice, stock or broth, thyme, cayenne, and pepper sauce. Cover pressure cooker and bring up to full pressure (15 pounds). Reduce heat to stabilize pressure and cook for 8 minutes. Release the pressure. Add the tomatoes, as much of the hot pepper as needed to suit your taste, the cilantro, and salt and pepper to taste. Heat briefly, if necessary, and serve with the bacon crumbled over the top.

CAPITOL BEAN SOUP

This is one of the most all-American soups ever, if only by virtue of the fact that it is served every single day in the Senate dining room of the Capitol. Recipes for it vary, even though they all claim to be the real McCoy. For its version, the Congressional Club cookbook lists only three ingredients—navy beans, water, and ham hocks.

This rendition is delicious, simple, and hearty. I like the final addition of fresh vegetables, although it is a pretty radical departure from what our elected officials enjoy in Washington, D.C. If you happen to have a ham bone on hand, use it in place of the ham hock.

Preparation time: 5 minutes plus soaking time
Pressure cooking time: 25 minutes

Yield: 5 cups

8 ounces Great Northern beans (or calico mixed dried beans)
4 cups water
1 large smoked ham hock
1 small onion, about 2 ounces, minced
1 medium stalk celery, minced
2 bay leaves
Salt and freshly ground black pepper to taste

1.   Soak the beans as directed (see Index). Drain well.

2.   Combine the beans, water, ham hock, onion, celery, and bay leaves in the pressure cooker. Cover pressure cooker and bring up to full pressure (15 pounds). Reduce heat to stabilize pressure and cook for 25 minutes. Release the pressure and remove the ham hock and bay leaves.

3.   With the back of a spoon, break up some of the beans to thicken the soup if desired. Dice the meat from the ham hock and add it to the soup along with salt and pepper to taste.

Note: If you want to add fresh vegetables, dice 2 medium carrots and 2 small stalks celery while the soup is cooking. Add them to the pressure cooker when you remove the ham hock. Cover pressure cooker and bring up to full pressure (15 pounds). Reduce heat to stabilize pressure and cook for 2 minutes. Finish as in step 3 above.

CHICKEN STOCK

If you use a lot of chicken, as most cooks do these days, in practically no time at all you can collect the chicken parts necessary to make stock. Keep them in the freezer until you've amassed the proper cache. Then, it's just a matter of adding a few vegetables and putting the stock up to cook when you have a bit of spare time.

One ingredient may raise a few eyebrows. Chicken feet are hardly common fare but they do make a marvelous addition to chicken stock. Buy them if you can, for you'll be rewarded with the richest stock ever.

Preparation time: 5 minutes
Pressure cooking time: 30 minutes

Yield: About 7 cups

2½ pounds chicken parts (backs, necks, wings, bones)
2 chicken feet (optional)
2 large carrots, cut into 1-inch pieces
1 large stalk celery, cut into 1-inch pieces
1 medium onion, unpeeled and quartered
4 whole peppercorns
8 cups water

1.   Put the chicken parts, chicken feet (if used), carrots, celery, onion, and peppercorns in a steamer basket and place in the pressure cooker. Add the water. Cover pressure cooker and bring up to full pressure (15 pounds). Reduce heat to stabilize pressure and cook for 30 minutes. Let pressure return to normal naturally. Remove the steamer basket and discard the bones and vegetables.

2.   Refrigerate the stock until the fat has solidified, then remove the fat. The stock can be refrigerated for up to 3 days or frozen.

BEEF STOCK

Roasting the bones gives the stock a deep, rich flavor, making it well worth the extra effort. To make an intensely flavored demi-glacé for sauces, boil the stock, uncovered, until it is reduced by one half or more.

Preparation time: 5 minutes
Pressure cooking time: 1½ hours
Other cooking time: 30 minutes

Yield: 6 cups

2½ pounds beef soup bones
1½ pounds beef shank bones
2 large carrots, cut into 1-inch pieces
2 medium stalks celery, cut into 1-inch pieces
1 large unpeeled onion, cut into 1-inch pieces
4 sprigs parsley
6 whole peppercorns
7 cups water

1.   Put the bones in a large shallow roasting pan. Strew the carrots, celery, and onion over the bones and bake in a preheated 450° F oven until the bones are browned, about 30 minutes.

2.   Transfer bones and vegetables to a steamer basket and add parsley and peppercorns. Place in pressure cooker and add 7 cups water. Be sure the water does not go beyond the maximum fill level in the pressure cooker. If it does, remove water until it reaches the recommended level. Cover pressure cooker and bring up to full pressure (15 pounds). Reduce heat to stabilize pressure and cook for 1½ hours.

3.   Let pressure drop on its own accord. Remove the steamer basket and discard the bones and vegetables. Refrigerate the stock overnight so the fat solidifies, then remove the fat. The stock can be refrigerated for up to 3 days or frozen.

4
MEATS AND POULTRY

BRAISED BEEFSTEAK WITH TEX-MEX
TOMATO SAUCE

COUNTRY KITCHEN SWISS STEAK

BEEF BRISKET WITH SMOKED CHILI SAUCE

GRANDMA MIN'S SWEDISH MEATBALLS

CORNED BEEF AND CABBAGE FEAST

OXTAILS WITH CHINESE FLAVOR

VEAL SHANKS WITH SAGE AND SUN-DRIED
TOMATO SAUCE

STUFFED VEAL BREAST

LAMB SHANKS WITH GARLICKY PORT
WINE SAUCE

TERIYAKI SPARERIBS

BARBECUED PORK CHOPS

PORK CHOPS STUFFED WITH APPLES
AND CORNBREAD

CHICKEN BREASTS WITH CREAMED LEEKS
AND MUSHROOMS

ITALIAN CHICKEN AND SAUSAGE WITH PEPPERS

RASPBERRY-GLAZED CHICKEN

CHICKEN IN VINEGAR

MUSTARD CHICKEN BREASTS WITH SPRING
VEGETABLES

CHICKEN WITH PROSCIUTTO AND MUSHROOMS

GOLDEN-GLAZED CHICKEN LITTLES

For all the talk about the changing American diet, ours essentially remains a meat-and-potatoes nation. A new awareness of nutrition reassures us that meat, even the red meats that have been maligned in the past, are OK to eat. That, of course, gives beef and pork eaters something to smile about. Portions may be smaller and certain cuts emphasized over others, but it's good to have these foods back on the table, without the onus of guilt to cloud our enjoyment of them.

The pressure cooker proves to be pretty remarkable when it comes to tackling meat cookery. Less expensive cuts of meat, which boast some of the best flavors around, are notorious for requiring lengthy cooking times. The pressure cooker will have no part of that, though. In minutes, not hours, even the most tenacious meats turn fork-tender. This means that cravings for lamb shanks need not go ignored, that an urge for corned beef can be acted upon.

No cook needs to be reminded of the virtues of chicken. With its long list of assets—economy; ease of preparation; versatility; low-fat, low-calorie content; and delectability—it's no surprise that this barnyard bird has become as popular as it is. It, too, is a good candidate for the pressure cooker. Chicken pieces cook up to tender, juicy perfection in under 10 minutes.

In all the recipes using chicken, I have suggested removing the skin before cooking, which considerably enhances its low-fat, low-calorie status. While a baked chicken may develop a nicely bronzed, crisp skin that waylays even the most ardent dieter, chicken cooked in the pressure cooker does not. The skin will always be soft and thus adds nothing to the character of the dish. And, with the skin removed, the meat will be infused with the flavors of the sauce, resulting in a tastier dish.

BRAISED BEEFSTEAK WITH TEX-MEX TOMATO SAUCE

Think of this as Swiss steak with a touch of Tex-Mex thrown in for good measure. It is a simple, homey dish that becomes lively under the influence of Mexican flavors. Serve with the sauce spooned over cooked white or brown rice.

Preparation time: 10 minutes
Pressure cooking time: 20 minutes
Other cooking time: 15 minutes

Yield: 3 to 4 servings

1 medium onion, about 5 ounces
2 poblano peppers
1 10-ounce can whole tomatoes with peppers
¼ cup flour
Salt and freshly ground black pepper to taste
1 top round beefsteak, about 1¼ pounds, cut ½-inch thick
1 tablespoon vegetable oil
1 tablespoon red wine vinegar
1 cup fresh cilantro leaves, minced

1.   Quarter the onion from top to bottom, then cut crosswise into slices. Dice the peppers. Drain the tomatoes, reserving the juice. Chop the tomatoes coarse and set aside.

2.   Combine the flour and salt and pepper to taste in a large plastic food bag. Add beefsteak and shake so the meat is evenly coated with flour.

3.   Heat the oil in pressure cooker over medium-high heat. Add beefsteak and sear quickly on both sides. Remove meat from pan and set aside.

4.   Add vinegar to pan and stir up the browned bits from the bottom of the pan. Add the onion and poblano peppers and cook for 1 minute. Add tomatoes with their juice.

5.   Return beefsteak to pan and spoon some of the vegetable mixture over the top. Cover pressure cooker and bring to full pressure (15 pounds). Reduce heat to stabilize pressure and cook for 20 minutes. Release pressure and set the meat aside. Boil the

sauce until it has thickened slightly, 7 to 9 minutes. Add the cilantro.

Note: If poblano peppers are not available, substitute 2 small green peppers and add minced fresh or canned serrano or jalapeño peppers to taste.

COUNTRY KITCHEN SWISS STEAK

This dish has homey, old-fashioned appeal with an updated twist. Instead of thickening the gravy with flour, pureed vegetables are used, lending a naturally sweet flavor and light finish.

Preparation time: 15 minutes
Pressure cooking time: 35 minutes
Other cooking time: 5 minutes

Yield: 4 servings

1 large onion, about 8 ounces
4 large carrots
1 tablespoon vegetable oil
1 chuck arm pot roast, about 2 pounds
2 tablespoons balsamic or red wine vinegar
1 cup beef stock or broth
1 bay leaf
2 large stalks celery
4 small parsnips, if desired
8 tiny or 4 small red potatoes
3 tablespoons tomato paste
Salt and freshly ground black pepper to taste

1.   Peel the onion and cut into wedges. Scrub two of the carrots and cut into 2-inch pieces.

2.   Heat the oil in the pressure cooker. Add the pot roast and brown well on both sides. Add the onion and the two cut carrots. Pour the vinegar into the bottom of the pan and add the stock or broth and bay leaf. Cover pressure cooker and bring up to full pressure (15 pounds). Reduce heat to stabilize pressure and cook for 30 minutes.

3.   While the roast is cooking, peel the remaining two carrots. Cut the carrots, celery, and parsnips, if used, into ¾-inch pieces. Cut the potatoes in half.

4.   When the roast has cooked 30 minutes, release pressure. Remove the meat, set aside, and cover to keep warm while you finish the sauce. Skim the fat from the cooking liquid (a gravy strainer is ideal) and remove the bay leaf. Spoon the carrots and onions into a blender and puree. Stir the puree into the cooking liquid. Return to the pressure cooker and add the tomato paste, vegetables, and salt and pepper to taste, mixing well.

5.   Cover pressure cooker and bring up to full pressure (15 pounds). Reduce heat to stabilize pressure and cook for 5 minutes. Transfer the roast to a platter and pour the sauce and vegetables over it.

BEEF BRISKET WITH SMOKED CHILI SAUCE

Though brisket is a wonderfully flavorful cut of meat, it is often bypassed by cooks who are in search of quicker meals. After all, oven cooking of brisket takes 4 to 5 hours. In the pressure cooker, the time is pared down to a much more reasonable 1 hour. Typically, brisket is flavored with tomatoes, as this one is, only this time it takes a walk on the wild side with a touch of Tex-Mex flavors.

If possible, cook the brisket a day or two ahead. This allows you to refrigerate the sauce, then easily remove the fat after it has solidified. The meat also slices much more neatly when it is cold. Reheat the meat in the sauce, either in a conventional oven or in a microwave oven.

Preparation time: 10 minutes
Pressure cooking time: 1 hour
Other cooking time: 5 minutes

Yield: 8 servings

3 large onions, about 1½ pounds total
1 tablespoon unsalted butter
1 16-ounce can Mexican-style stewed tomatoes
1 to 2 chipotle peppers packed in adobo sauce, drained (but
*   reserving 1 to 2 tablespoons sauce) and chopped coarse*
3 tablespoons light brown sugar
1 teaspoon ground cumin
1 well-trimmed 3- to 4-pound beef brisket

1.   Peel the onions, cut in half lengthwise, and cut into thin wedges. Melt the butter in pressure cooker. Add onions and cook over medium-high heat, stirring often, until they begin to soften, about 4 minutes.

2.   Add the tomatoes with their liquid, chipotles and their sauce, brown sugar, and cumin and mix well. Add the brisket and spoon some of the onion-tomato mixture over the meat. Cover pressure cooker and bring up to full pressure (15 pounds). Reduce heat to stabilize pressure and cook for 1 hour. Release pressure.

3.   Remove brisket and set aside. To serve immediately, skim as much fat from the sauce as possible. Cut the meat against the grain into thin slices and serve with the sauce. Or, for do-ahead, wrap the brisket separately from the sauce and refrigerate overnight. About 40 minutes before serving, remove meat from refrigerator and cut against the grain into thin slices. Transfer to a shallow casserole. Skim the solidified fat from the sauce. Reheat the meat and sauce in preheated 350° F oven until hot, 25 to 30 minutes.

Note: Chipotle peppers are smoked jalapeños. They are most readily available in cans, packed in adobo sauce. Usually, they are pretty potent as far as heat goes. Taste a little bit of the sauce before deciding how many of the peppers and how much sauce to add. If you can't get chipotles, use fresh jalapeños and add several dashes of liquid smoke.

GRANDMA MIN'S SWEDISH MEATBALLS

The taste and light texture of these delicately flavored meatballs stand as a testament to old-fashioned Swedish goodness. In the interest of reducing calories and fat, you can use half-and-half in place of the cream or leave it out altogether. Taste the gravy before adding it and add as much or as little as you like. Serve over rice or buttered noodles.

Preparation time: 10 minutes plus 1 hour chilling time
Pressure cooking time: 10 minutes
Other cooking time: 2 minutes

Yield: 4 to 6 servings

1 large egg
1 cup milk
½ cup stale bread crumbs
1⅓ pounds meatloaf mix (equal parts ground pork, beef,
    and veal)
1 small onion, about 2 ounces, minced
½ teaspoon salt
1¼ teaspoons dried dill weed
⅛ teaspoon ground cardamom
⅛ teaspoon ground allspice
⅛ teaspoon freshly grated nutmeg plus more to taste, if desired
3 tablespoons unsalted butter
⅓ cup flour
1½ cups beef stock or broth
Salt and freshly ground black pepper to taste
½ cup whipping cream

1.   Beat the egg in a medium bowl. Add the milk and bread crumbs and mix well. Add the meatloaf mix, onion, salt, ¼ teaspoon dill, cardamom, allspice, and ⅛ teaspoon nutmeg. Mix with your hands until well blended. Cover and refrigerate 1 hour.

2.   With lightly floured hands, shape meat mixture into 16 meatballs.

3.   Melt butter in pressure cooker and stir in flour. Cook, stirring constantly, 1 minute. Add stock or broth, remaining 1 teaspoon

dill, and salt and pepper to taste, plus freshly grated nutmeg if desired. Stir until smooth. Carefully add meatballs. Cover pressure cooker and bring up to full pressure (15 pounds). Reduce heat to stabilize pressure and cook for 10 minutes. Release pressure and add cream, shaking pan and gently stirring so cream is well blended into sauce. Heat, if necessary, without letting the sauce come to a boil.

CORNED BEEF AND CABBAGE FEAST

It could be the luck of the Irish or it could be the time-saving grace of the pressure cooker. Four hours of cooking is pared down to one for a meltingly tender corned beef brisket. You can add whatever vegetables suit your fancy or, if the corned beef is slated for sandwiches, you can elect to add none at all. There's plenty of meat here, enough for a hearty meal and then the requisite leftovers— corned beef hash or sandwiches.

Preparation time: 20 minutes
Pressure cooking time: 1 hour

Yield: 6 to 8 servings

1 corned beef brisket, about 4 pounds
1 medium onion, quartered
1 tablespoon pickling spice
Water, about 12 cups
1 medium head cabbage, cut in wedges
6 to 8 small red potatoes, peeled
Carrots, parsnips, or rutabaga, as desired, cut into 1-inch
*   chunks*

Creamy Horseradish Sauce (*if desired*)

½ cup whipping cream
2 teaspoons prepared horseradish or to taste
1½ teaspoons Dijon mustard
½ teaspoon red wine vinegar
Salt to taste

1.   Combine the corned beef, onion, and pickling spice in the pressure cooker. Add water to cover, making sure it does not go beyond the recommended level for the pressure cooker. Cover pressure cooker and bring up to full pressure (15 pounds). Because of the large amount of water, it will take about 15 minutes to reach full pressure. Reduce heat to stabilize pressure and cook for 1 hour. Release pressure.

2.   Remove the corned beef and set aside. Add the cabbage, potatoes, and any other vegetables you are using. Cover pressure cooker and bring up to full pressure (15 pounds). When full pressure is reached, stop the cooking and release pressure. The vegetables should all be properly tender.

3.   To make the horseradish sauce, whip the cream with an electric mixer until it holds soft peaks, then fold in the remaining ingredients. The sauce can be made several hours in advance and refrigerated.

4.   Cut the corned beef into thin slices, going against the grain. Serve with the vegetables and horseradish sauce, if desired.

OXTAILS WITH CHINESE FLAVOR

Oxtails are largely overlooked, partly because they normally require 3 hours of cooking for the recalcitrant meat to turn fork-tender. The pressure cooker speeds up the clock considerably so this succulent cut of meat can be enjoyed more often—and more quickly.

Here, oxtails are infused with light Oriental flavors, in marked contrast to the heartier flavors they're usually paired with. The pan juices are delicious poured over Oriental udon noodles or vermicelli. Chinese vegetables such as bamboo shoots and water chestnuts can be added to the juices after cooking if you wish.

Preparation time: 10 minutes plus 12 hours marinating time
Pressure cooking time: 35 minutes
Other cooking time: 5 minutes

Yield: 2 to 3 servings

1 large clove garlic
1 piece fresh ginger, about ¾-inch cube
⅓ cup dry sherry
¼ cup vegetable oil
¼ cup seasoned rice vinegar
1 teaspoon sugar
1 teaspoon Oriental sesame oil
2¼ pounds oxtails
¼ cup chicken stock or broth
Salt to taste

1.   Mince the garlic and ginger. Place in a large plastic food bag and add sherry, 3 tablespoons vegetable oil, vinegar, sugar, and sesame oil. Mix well and add oxtails. Seal bag and refrigerate 12 hours.

2.   Heat remaining tablespoon vegetable oil in pressure cooker. Remove oxtails from marinade, letting excess drip off. Reserve marinade. Add oxtails to hot oil and brown on all sides. Add reserved marinade and chicken stock or broth.

3.   Cover pressure cooker and bring up to full pressure (15 pounds). Reduce heat to stabilize pressure and cook for 35 minutes. Release pressure. Remove oxtails with tongs and set aside. Pour pan juices into a gravy strainer and pour off fat or carefully spoon off as much fat as possible. Add salt to taste. Pour skimmed sauce over oxtails.

Note: Seasoned rice vinegar, also called sushi vinegar, is Oriental rice vinegar that is seasoned with sugar and salt. It is sold in many large supermarkets and specialty food stores. If it is not available, use plain rice vinegar or white wine vinegar instead and add sugar and salt to taste.

VEAL SHANKS WITH SAGE
AND SUN-DRIED TOMATO SAUCE

Veal shanks, also called ossobucco, have a wonderful, rich flavor and meltingly soft texture. Here, they're partnered with a light sauce that uses two types of tomatoes—fresh plum tomatoes for texture, sun-dried tomatoes for an intense flavor. Serve the sauce over rice or noodles.

Preparation time: 10 minutes
Pressure cooking time: 30 minutes
Other cooking time: 10 minutes

Yield: 2 servings

2 tablespoons olive oil
2 veal shanks, about 1 pound each
¼ cup dry white wine
1 small onion, about 3 ounces, thinly sliced
1 large clove garlic, thinly sliced
3 plum tomatoes, about 8 ounces total, peeled and chopped coarse
¼ cup minced sun-dried tomatoes
1 teaspoon rubbed sage
½ teaspoon minced orange zest
½ cup veal or chicken stock or chicken broth

1.   Heat the oil in the pressure cooker. Add the veal shanks and brown well on all sides. Set aside on a plate.

2.   Slowly pour the wine into the hot pan, stirring up any brown bits from the bottom. Add the onion and garlic and cook 1 minute. Add the plum and sun-dried tomatoes, sage, orange zest, and stock or broth, then the shanks.

3.   Cover pressure cooker and bring up to full pressure (15 pounds). Reduce heat to stabilize pressure and cook for 30 minutes. Release pressure and remove the shanks. Boil the sauce vigorously, uncovered, for 8 to 10 minutes to thicken.

STUFFED VEAL BREAST

A small veal breast is convenient and easy to handle. If you purchase a larger one, add an additional 10 to 12 minutes of cooking time for each extra pound.

Preparation time: 20 minutes
Pressure cooking time: 40 minutes
Other cooking time: 15 minutes

Yield: 3 to 4 servings

3 ounces salt pork
1 medium onion, about 4 ounces
1 small red bell pepper, about 4 ounces, seeded
4 ounces small mushrooms
1 10-ounce package frozen leaf spinach, thawed
½ teaspoon dried sage
¼ teaspoon freshly grated nutmeg
Salt and freshly ground black pepper to taste
2 slices day-old bread
¼ cup milk
1 small (3½- to 4-pound) veal breast, with a pocket cut for stuffing
2 tablespoons unsalted butter
¾ cup chicken stock or broth
½ cup white port or other dry white wine
2 bay leaves

1.   Rinse the salt pork, cut off and discard the rind, and dice. Dice the onion. Put the onion and salt pork in the pressure cooker and cook gently over medium heat, stirring often, until the fat is rendered from the pork and the onion is soft, about 5 minutes.

2.   Dice the red pepper. Trim and discard the stems from the mushrooms and quarter the caps. Squeeze the spinach firmly to remove as much moisture as possible. Add these vegetables to the pressure cooker along with the sage, nutmeg, and salt and pepper to taste. *Be careful adding salt since the salt pork may add enough salt to the stuffing.* Cook over medium heat until the mushrooms are soft, about 5 minutes. Remove from heat and set aside.

3.   Coarsely crumble the bread and combine in a small dish with the milk. Stir well so the milk is absorbed. Add the bread to the above mixture.

4.   Open the pocket of the veal breast with your hands and spoon in the stuffing. Tie the breast closed in several places with kitchen twine.

5.   Wipe out the pressure cooker. Melt the butter in the pressure cooker and brown the breast. Add the stock or broth, port, and bay leaves. Cover pressure cooker and bring up to full pressure (15 pounds). Reduce heat to stabilize pressure and cook for 40 minutes. Release pressure and let the meat stand for 10 minutes. Untie the breast and cut into portions, following the ribs.

LAMB SHANKS WITH GARLICKY
PORT WINE SAUCE

Lamb shanks are a wonderful cut of meat, full of rich, hearty flavor. Those who are accustomed to cooking them for 2 hours will be quite surprised at how meltingly tender and succulent they are after just 30 minutes in the pressure cooker. The sauce is robust and richly flavored, an apt partner to the meat. Don't be daunted by the amount of garlic. The cloves become quite sweet and tame as they cook. Serve the sauce over cooked rice, orzo, or other tiny pasta.

Preparation time: 10 minutes
Pressure cooking time: 30 minutes
Additional cooking time: 10 minutes

Yield: 2 servings

2 lamb shanks, about 1 pound each
Salt and freshly ground black pepper to taste
1 tablespoon olive oil
10 cloves garlic, peeled and left whole
½ cup chicken stock or broth
½ cup port wine
1 tablespoon tomato paste
½ teaspoon dried rosemary
1 tablespoon unsalted butter
1 to 2 teaspoons balsamic vinegar

1.   Trim excess fat from the lamb shanks and season them with salt and pepper to taste. Heat the oil in the pressure cooker. Add the shanks and brown on all sides. When they are almost completely browned, add the garlic cloves and cook until they are lightly browned but not burned. Add the stock or broth, port, tomato paste, and rosemary, stirring so the tomato paste dissolves.

2.   Close the pressure cooker and bring up to full pressure (15 pounds). Reduce heat to stabilize pressure and cook for 30 minutes.

3.   Release pressure and remove the lamb shanks. Return the pressure cooker to the stove. Boil, uncovered, for 5 minutes to reduce and thicken the sauce. Whisk in the butter, then add the vinegar. Serve the sauce over the lamb shanks.

TERIYAKI SPARERIBS

Cooking spareribs is almost always a two-step preparation. First, they're boiled to remove some of the fat and to tenderize them. Then, they're grilled to finish them off with a smoky flavor. The pressure cooker does a marvelous job of tenderizing the ribs, quickly bringing them to the fall-off-the-bone stage. Then, while still warm, they're placed in an Oriental marinade until you're ready to put them on the grill.

Preparation time: 5 minutes plus 12 to 24 hours marinating time
Pressure cooking time: 15 minutes
Grilling time: About 10 minutes

Yield: 3 to 4 servings

3 pounds pork spareribs
Water, about 10 cups
½ cup light brown sugar
⅓ cup dark soy sauce
⅓ cup catsup
¼ cup hoisin sauce
2 tablespoons dry sherry

1.   Cut the spareribs into serving-size pieces. Place in the pressure cooker and add enough water to cover them, making sure the water does not go beyond the recommended level of the pressure cooker. Cover pressure cooker and bring up to full pressure (15 pounds). Reduce heat to stabilize pressure and cook for 15 minutes. Release pressure and remove ribs from pan to cool slightly.

2.   Combine sugar, soy sauce, catsup, hoisin sauce, and sherry in a large plastic food bag. Add ribs and turn them over several times so they are well coated with the marinade. Refrigerate for 12 to 24 hours.

3.   Prepare a hot grill, preferably with a mix of charcoal and mesquite wood. Remove ribs from marinade and let excess drip off. Place ribs around outer edge of coals so they do not cook too fast. Grill until they are browned on both sides, brushing several times with the reserved marinade.

BARBECUED PORK CHOPS

While we've come to accept barbecued to mean cooked outdoors on a grill, in the deep South it also means meat cooked in a rich, spicy, red barbecue sauce. Here, then, is a Southern-style barbecue of pork chops bathed in a lip-smacking sauce.

Preparation time: 10 minutes
Pressure cooking time: 15 minutes
Other cooking time: 10 minutes

Yield: 4 servings

¼ cup flour
1 teaspoon chili powder
Salt and freshly ground black pepper to taste
4 butterflied pork chops
1 tablespoon vegetable oil
2 tablespoons cider vinegar
1 small onion, about 2 ounces, minced
½ cup tomato sauce
2 tablespoons light brown sugar
2½ teaspoons Dijon mustard
2½ teaspoons Worcestershire sauce
1 teaspoon Hungarian paprika
½ teaspoon ground clove

1.   Combine the flour, chili powder, and salt and pepper to taste in a large paper bag. Add the pork chops and shake them so they are evenly coated with flour.

2.   Heat 1½ teaspoons oil in the pressure cooker. Add two of the pork chops and brown well on both sides. Set aside and add the remaining oil. Brown the other pork chops and set aside. Add the vinegar to the pan and then the onion, tomato sauce, brown sugar, mustard, Worcestershire sauce, paprika, and clove. Return the pork chops, turning them over once so they are coated with the sauce mixture. Cover pressure cooker and bring up to full pressure (15 pounds). Reduce heat to stabilize pressure and cook for 15 minutes. Release pressure. To serve, place pork chops on serving plate and top with sauce.

PORK CHOPS STUFFED WITH APPLES
AND CORNBREAD

Extra-thick-cut pork chops are filled with a savory mix of corn-bread, apples, bacon, and herbs, then simmered in broth until they become fork-tender. Be sure to buy chops that are at least 1 inch thick so a pocket can easily be cut into them.

Preparation time: 10 minutes
Pressure cooking time: 15 minutes
Other cooking time: 10 minutes

Yield: 4 servings

2 strips bacon
1 small onion, about 2 ounces
1 small stalk celery
½ small Granny Smith or other tart apple
1 cup packaged cornbread stuffing mix
1 large egg, beaten lightly
¼ teaspoon dried sage
Freshly grated nutmeg to taste
Salt and freshly ground black pepper to taste
2 to 3 tablespoons liquid (cream, apple juice, or chicken stock), as
    needed
4 thick-cut pork chops
1 tablespoon vegetable oil
1 tablespoon unsalted butter
½ cup chicken stock or broth

1.   Dice bacon, onion, celery, and apple.

2.   Brown bacon in the pressure cooker. Spill off all but 1 table-spoon fat and add the onion and celery. Cook until softened, about 2 minutes. Transfer to a medium bowl and add the apple, stuffing mix, egg, sage, nutmeg, and salt and pepper to taste. Mix well. Add enough liquid to moisten the crumbs. The stuffing should be moist but not wet.

3.   Trim excess fat from the pork chops. Cut a pocket through each, going all the way to the bone. Fill each pocket with stuffing. Press to close. Season outside of chops with more salt and pepper to taste.

4.   Heat the oil and butter in the pressure cooker. Add the pork chops and brown well on both sides. Pour the stock or broth into the bottom of the pan rather than over the chops. Cover pressure cooker and bring up to full pressure (15 pounds). Reduce heat to stabilize pressure and cook for 15 minutes. Release pressure. Remove pork chops from liquid and serve hot.

CHICKEN BREASTS WITH CREAMED LEEKS AND MUSHROOMS

Ease and elegance are not mutually exclusive, as this dish so aptly proves. Chicken breasts are poached at the same time leeks are steamed—all in just minutes. An extra step of flattening the chicken breasts ensures that they cook evenly and quickly.

Preparation time: 10 minutes plus 30 minutes soaking time
Pressure cooking time: 2 minutes
Other cooking time: 5 minutes

Yield: 4 servings

¼ ounce imported dried mushrooms, such as porcini
⅓ cup hot water
4 large leeks, about 2 pounds total
4 boneless chicken breast halves
1 cup chicken stock or broth
2 tablespoons white port or other white wine
1 teaspoon Dijon mustard
⅓ cup whipping cream
Freshly grated nutmeg to taste
Salt and freshly ground black pepper to taste

1.   Put mushrooms in a small dish and cover with hot water. Let soak until soft, about 30 minutes. Drain and slice the mushrooms.

2.   Trim the coarse green ends from the leeks. Slit the leeks and fan the leaves open under cold water to remove the dirt. Quarter them lengthwise, then cut crosswise into ½-inch slices. Place in the steamer basket of pressure cooker.

3.   Remove the skin from the chicken. Pound each breast between 2 sheets of waxed paper or plastic wrap to a uniform thickness of about ¼ inch.

4.   Combine chicken stock or broth and port wine in the pressure cooker. Add chicken breasts. Place the steamer basket over the breasts. Cover pressure cooker and bring up to full pressure (15 pounds). Reduce heat to stabilize pressure and cook for 2 minutes. Release pressure and remove steamer basket. Set chicken aside and tent it with aluminum foil.

5.   Remove all but ¼ cup of the cooking liquid from the bottom of the pressure cooker. Add mushrooms and mustard and heat to a boil. Add cream and cook over high heat until it thickens slightly, 2 to 3 minutes. Add leeks, nutmeg, and salt and pepper to taste and remove from heat. To serve, spoon leeks onto serving plates and top with a chicken breast.

ITALIAN CHICKEN AND SAUSAGE
WITH PEPPERS

Lusty and full-flavored, this is a perfect dish for Sunday night suppers or casual entertaining. Instead of serving rice or pasta with it, try a big, crusty loaf of Italian bread, which is perfect for sopping up every last bit of the sauce.

Preparation time: 10 minutes
Pressure cooking time: 10 minutes
Other cooking time: 15 minutes

Yield: 4 to 6 servings

1 tablespoon olive oil
4 Italian link sausages, about 12 ounces total
1 frying chicken, skin removed, cut into serving pieces
1 medium onion, about 4 ounces
2 medium green bell peppers, about 10 ounces total
2 large cloves garlic
2 tablespoons red wine vinegar
1 16-ounce can diced tomatoes, drained
¾ teaspoon dried basil
¼ teaspoon fennel seeds
Crushed red pepper flakes to taste
Salt and freshly ground black pepper to taste

1.   Heat the oil in the pressure cooker. Prick the skin of the sausages in several places with the tines of a fork. Add the sausages and chicken to the oil and cook until well browned on all sides.

2.   While the chicken is cooking, dice the onion. Cut the green peppers into ¾-inch-thick strips. Mince the garlic.

3.   When the chicken and sausages are browned, remove them from the pan and set aside. Add the onion, green peppers, and garlic to the pan and cook, stirring often, until they begin to soften, about 4 minutes. Add the vinegar and stir up the browned bits from the bottom of the pan. Add the chicken and sausages, tomatoes, basil, fennel, red pepper flakes, and salt and pepper to taste. Cover pressure cooker and bring up to full pressure (15 pounds). Reduce heat to stabilize pressure and cook for 10 minutes. Release pressure and adjust the seasoning.

RASPBERRY-GLAZED CHICKEN

A triple dose of a hearty raspberry-and-red-wine sauce gives chicken a marvelously robust flavor. First, the chicken is marinated in the sauce, then cooked in it, and finally glazed with it for a finger-licking-good finish.

Preparation time: 5 minutes plus 4 hours marinating time
Pressure cooking time: 12 minutes
Other cooking time: 15 minutes

Yield: 3 to 4 servings

½ cup light, fruity red wine
½ cup raspberry vinegar
¼ cup dark soy sauce
2 tablespoons honey
1 teaspoon Dijon mustard
1 medium clove garlic, minced
1 frying chicken, cut into serving pieces

1. Combine the wine, vinegar, soy sauce, honey, mustard, and garlic in a large plastic food bag. Remove the skin and fat from the chicken. Add the chicken to the marinade, seal the bag, and turn it over several times so the chicken is well coated with marinade. Refrigerate at least 4 hours or overnight.

2. Transfer the chicken and marinade to the pressure cooker. Cover pressure cooker and bring up to full pressure (15 pounds). Reduce heat to stabilize pressure and cook for 12 minutes. Release pressure. Remove the chicken and set aside, leaving the marinade in the pan. Skim any fat from the surface of the liquid, then boil vigorously, uncovered, until thick and syrupy, 10 to 12 minutes. Return the chicken to the pan, turn it over several times so it is coated with the glaze, and cook 2 minutes. Serve immediately.

Note: Raspberry vinegar is available in some supermarkets and specialty food stores, or it can easily be made at home during raspberry season. To make raspberry vinegar, put 1 cup of raspberries in a clean glass jar with a tight-fitting lid. Add 2 cups of white wine vinegar, cover, and let stand 10 days before using. The berries can either be strained out, taking care not to crush them into the vinegar, or left in the vinegar.

CHICKEN IN VINEGAR

Chicken in vinegar is a classic dish of the French countryside. While it rarely is seen on the menus of three-star restaurants, it almost always shows up in bistros and brasseries, where the food is rustic and homey.

Preparation time: 10 minutes
Pressure cooking time: 10 minutes
Other cooking time: 10 minutes

Yield: 3 to 4 servings

2 large shallots
2 medium tomatoes, about 8 ounces total
6 chicken thighs
3 tablespoons unsalted butter
3 tablespoons red wine vinegar
⅓ cup dry white wine
⅓ cup chicken stock or broth
½ teaspoon dried tarragon
¼ teaspoon salt
Freshly ground black pepper to taste

1.   Mince the shallots. Cut the tomatoes in half crosswise and squeeze gently to remove the seeds. Dice the tomatoes. Remove the skin from the chicken and trim the excess fat.

2.   Melt 1 tablespoon butter in the pressure cooker. Add the chicken and brown on both sides. Remove from the pan and set aside.

3.   Add the vinegar to the pan and scrape any browned bits from the bottom of the pan so they dissolve into the sauce. Add the shallots and cook until they soften, about 2 minutes, stirring constantly. Add the tomatoes, wine, stock or broth, tarragon, salt, and pepper to taste, then arrange the chicken over the top. Cover pressure cooker and bring up to full pressure (15 pounds). Reduce heat to stabilize pressure and cook for 10 minutes. Release pressure and remove the chicken.

4.   Increase the heat to high and boil the sauce until it thickens slightly, about 5 minutes. Stir in the remaining 2 tablespoons butter and adjust the seasoning.

MUSTARD CHICKEN BREASTS WITH
SPRING VEGETABLES

A tangle of fresh vegetables provides a colorful cushion for tender boneless chicken breasts. It's a quick meal to prepare, yet still comes across with a lot of pizzazz. Asparagus spears, red or yellow pepper strips, or snow peas can be tossed in with the other vegetables, all depending on what looks best at the market. Just be sure to cut the tender vegetables slightly larger than the harder ones, such as carrots.

Preparation time: 10 minutes
Pressure cooking time: 4 minutes

Yield: 2 servings

1 medium zucchini
1 medium carrot, peeled
1 medium leek, coarse green ends trimmed
2 boneless chicken breast halves
1½ tablespoons unsalted butter
1 teaspoon Dijon or honey mustard
1½ teaspoons fresh lemon juice
½ teaspoon dried tarragon
Salt and freshly ground black pepper to taste
1 cup water

1.   Cut the zucchini, carrot, and leek into thin matchstick juliennes, about 2 inches long. Cut the carrot somewhat thinner than the leek and zucchini so they all cook in the same amount of time. Put the vegetables into the steamer basket of the pressure cooker and toss together.

2.   Remove the skin from the chicken breasts. Pound between plastic wrap or waxed paper to a uniform thickness of about ¼ inch.

3.   Melt the butter and mix with the mustard, lemon juice, tarragon, and salt and pepper to taste. Brush part of the mixture over both sides of the chicken breasts and place the breasts over the vegetables. Reserve the rest of the butter mixture for the vegetables.

4.   Add 1 cup water to the bottom of the pressure cooker and heat

to a boil. Insert the trivet and then the steamer basket. Cover pressure cooker and bring up to full pressure (15 pounds). Reduce heat to stabilize pressure and cook for 4 minutes. Release pressure immediately and set the chicken aside. Toss the vegetables with the remaining butter mixture and additional salt and pepper if desired. Divide vegetables between 2 plates and top with a breast half.

CHICKEN WITH PROSCIUTTO AND MUSHROOMS

Almost all of the world's cuisines use chicken in one way or another. Because of its international popularity, there are scores of different ways to approach this most versatile bird. This Italian interpretation uses the rich taste of prosciutto in tandem with a mix of herbs to enhance the mild taste of chicken.

Preparation time: 15 minutes
Pressure cooking time: 8 minutes
Other cooking time: 8 minutes

Yield: 3 to 4 servings

1 3-ounce slice prosciutto
1 tablespoon olive oil
4 ounces mushrooms, quartered
1 frying chicken, cut into serving pieces
1 small onion, about 3 ounces
1 large clove garlic
1 medium tomato, about 6 ounces
¼ cup dry white wine
¼ cup chicken stock or broth
1 tablespoon tomato paste
1 teaspoon dried sage
1 teaspoon dried rosemary
2 bay leaves
12 whole peppercorns, crushed coarse
Salt and freshly ground black pepper to taste

1.   Cut the prosciutto into small cubes. Heat the oil in the pressure cooker. Add prosciutto and cook over medium heat for 2 minutes. Add mushrooms and cook until they are almost tender, about 5 minutes. Transfer to a small dish.

2.   Remove the skin from the chicken. Cut the onion into thin wedges. Mince the garlic. Core the tomato, cut in half crosswise and squeeze gently to remove the seeds, then dice.

3.   Add the chicken, onion, garlic, wine, stock or broth, tomato paste, sage, rosemary, bay leaves, and peppercorns to the pressure cooker. Cover pressure cooker and bring up to full pressure (15 pounds). Reduce heat to stabilize pressure and cook for 8 minutes. Release pressure and add the mushrooms, prosciutto, and tomato. Taste, and add salt and more pepper if desired.

GOLDEN-GLAZED CHICKEN LITTLES

Chicken drumsticks are terrific finger food, whether they're slated for a buffet party or beachside picnic. This sweet and saucy version, flavored with an unexpected mix of ingredients, wins high marks.

Preparation time: 5 minutes plus 4 hours marinating time
Pressure cooking time: 10 minutes
Other cooking time: 15 minutes
Yield: 4 main dish servings or more as an appetizer

1 small clove garlic
1 small piece fresh ginger, about ¾-inch cube
5 tablespoons honey
¼ cup mango chutney
3 tablespoons dark soy sauce
3 tablespoons dry sherry
1 tablespoon rice wine vinegar or white wine vinegar
2½ to 3 pounds chicken drumsticks, skin removed

1.   Mince the garlic and ginger. Transfer to the pressure cooker and add the honey, chutney, soy sauce, sherry, and vinegar and mix well. Add the chicken drumsticks and turn them over so they are well coated with the sauce.

2.   Cover pressure cooker and bring up to full pressure (15 pounds). Reduce heat to stabilize pressure and cook for 10 minutes. Release pressure and allow to cool slightly. Transfer the drumsticks and any sauce to a large plastic food bag, seal tightly, and turn over several times so the chicken is well coated. Refrigerate 4 hours or overnight.

3.   Line a jelly roll pan with aluminum foil. Heat oven to 350° F. Arrange the drumsticks on the pan and brush with any remaining sauce. Bake, turning once, until they are thickly coated with sauce, 10 to 15 minutes. Serve warm or at room temperature.

5
STEWS AND ONE-DISH MEALS

■

GRAND CHAMP CHILI

GREEK BEEF STEW

MY VERSION OF ROY DE GROOT'S
HUNGARIAN GOULASH

WINTER BEEF AND VEGETABLE STEW

CURRIED BEEF

BEEF STROGANOFF

MEXICAN MEATBALL STEW WITH VEGETABLES

VEAL RAGOUT WITH DILLED CARROTS

LAMB AND FETA STUFFED PEPPERS

GREEN CHILE PORK AND HOMINY STEW

SPANISH PAELLA

JAMBALAYA

For all the talk about how stews and casseroles are making a big comeback, it's pretty hard to find evidence of it. Despite the homey comfort that distinguishes them, the reality of stews is that they require long, slow cooking—using conventional methods. Fortunately, stews just happen to be one of the things that the pressure cooker does especially well—and especially quickly.

Much of the success of stews depends on using inexpensive cuts of meat. Through cooking, the meat becomes exquisitely tender and at the same time infuses the sauce with marvelously rich flavor and wonderful body. In the oven or in a conventional stovetop pot, it can take anywhere from 2 to 3 hours for stew meat to become tender. That, of course, scratches stews off the weekday menu for many people. The pressure cooker, on the other hand, accomplishes the same goals with astonishing efficiency. In most instances, stews are table-ready in less than 30 minutes.

Many of the stews that follow involve a two-step cooking process, which is typical for stews no matter how they are cooked. First, the meat is browned in fat, then the remaining ingredients (except for some of the more tender vegetables) are added, and the pot is put on to cook for the bulk of its cooking time. If you're following a reduced-fat diet, you can eliminate the browning of the meat and hence the extra fat that is added for that purpose. Or, with extra-careful cooking, you can reduce the amount of fat used to brown the meat. In any event, you will still be rewarded with a richly flavored stew.

GRAND CHAMP CHILI

Chili doesn't need long, slow simmering to pack a good punch. In the pressure cooker, the flavors develop just as though the chili had simmered on the back burner for hours. This version is chock-full of beans and meat, which are accented with a mildly assertive mix of spices. Add more or less chili powder and jalapeños as your taste dictates. Ground turkey can be used in place of beef for a lighter and leaner version.

Preparation time: 15 minutes
Pressure cooking time: 15 minutes
Other cooking: 5 minutes

Yield: About 9 cups

2 medium onions, about 10 ounces total
3 medium cloves garlic
1½ pounds lean, coarsely ground beef, preferably round or sirloin
   steak
1 small red bell pepper, about 4 ounces
1 small green bell pepper, about 4 ounces
5 jalapeño peppers, seeded as desired
2 tablespoons chili powder
1 teaspoon cumin seeds
½ teaspoon cayenne pepper
3 tablespoons light brown sugar
1 6-ounce can tomato paste
1 28-ounce can crushed tomatoes in tomato sauce
1½ cups beef stock or broth
1 16-ounce can kidney beans, drained and rinsed
1 16-ounce can pinto beans, drained and rinsed
Garnishes (sour cream, shredded cheese, sliced green onions, or
   fresh, minced cilantro)

1.   Mince the onions and garlic. Brown the meat with the onions and garlic in pressure cooker. Pour off any accumulated fat.

2.   Dice the red and green bell peppers and mince the jalapeño peppers. Add them to the pan along with the chili powder, cumin seeds, cayenne pepper, and brown sugar. Stir and cook 1 minute. Add the tomato paste, crushed tomatoes and their liquid, and the stock or broth. Cover the pan and bring to full pressure (15 pounds). Reduce heat to stabilize pressure and cook for 15 minutes.

3.   Release pressure and stir in the kidney beans and pinto beans. Serve with garnishes of your choice. The chili can be made in advance and refrigerated for up to 4 days or frozen.

Note: With the seeds and ribs removed, jalapeño peppers are fairly mild. Add the seeds from one or two of the peppers to give the chili a spicy edge.

GREEK BEEF STEW

An aromatic mix of herbs and spices lends a unique and special flavor to this traditional Greek stew known as stifado. In practically no time, the meat is fork-tender and the flavors blended to a wonderful complexity. Like all stews, it tastes even better when it is reheated, so you can plan on making it ahead if that suits your schedule. Orzo, a tiny Greek pasta that looks much like rice, is a great accompaniment and so, too, is rice.

Preparation time: 15 minutes
Pressure cooking time: 20 minutes
Other cooking time: 10 minutes

Yield: 4 servings

1½ tablespoons olive oil
1½ pounds lean beef chuck, cut in 1½-inch cubes
10 ounces small white boiling onions, peeled
1 large clove garlic, minced
¼ cup port wine
¼ cup tomato paste
½ cup beef stock or broth
2 tablespoons red wine vinegar
1½ tablespoons light brown sugar
1 bay leaf
½ teaspoon ground cumin
½ teaspoon dried oregano
¼ teaspoon cinnamon
¼ teaspoon dried rosemary
⅛ teaspoon ground clove
Salt and freshly ground black pepper to taste

1.   Heat the oil in the pressure cooker. Add half the beef and cook until well browned. Remove with a slotted spoon and set aside. Brown the remaining meat and set aside.

2.   Add onions and garlic to pan and cook 1 minute. Add port and stir up any browned bits from the bottom of the pan. Add all the remaining ingredients, including the meat, stirring well so the tomato paste dissolves. Cover pressure cooker and bring up to full

pressure (15 pounds). Reduce heat to stabilize pressure and cook for 20 minutes. Release pressure and adjust seasoning. The stew can be refrigerated for several days or frozen. Reheat on the stove or in the microwave oven.

MY VERSION OF ROY DE GROOT'S HUNGARIAN GOULASH

In the early 1970s, long after most pressure cookers had been stowed away in attics and basements, Roy de Groot wrote *Pressure Cookery Perfected*, a cookbook extolling the virtues of having a pressure cooker in a modern kitchen. A marvelously gifted cook with a number of cookbooks already under his belt, de Groot brought a new stylishness to pressure cookery. This recipe is adapted from his pressure cooker cookbook. It is robust and well flavored. Serve it in soup bowls with plenty of French bread for soaking up the gravy.

Preparation time: 15 minutes
Pressure cooking time: 12 minutes
Other cooking time: 10 minutes

Yield: 6 servings

2 ounces salt pork
1 tablespoon unsalted butter
2 pounds beef rump, cut into 1½-inch cubes
2 large onions, about 1 pound total
6 small red potatoes, about 8 to 9 ounces total
2 medium green bell peppers, about 12 ounces total
½ cup dry white wine
3 tablespoons tomato paste
4 teaspoons Hungarian paprika
Salt and freshly ground black pepper to taste
1 cup sour cream
1½ teaspoons caraway seeds

1.   Dice the salt pork. Melt the butter in the pressure cooker. Add the salt pork and cook until brown and crisp. Add the beef and brown lightly on all sides.

2.   Meanwhile, peel the onions and cut them into wedges. Peel the potatoes and cut in half. Cut the green peppers into 1-inch squares. Add the onions, potatoes, and green peppers to the pan. Stir together the wine, tomato paste, paprika, and salt and pepper to taste and add to the pressure cooker.

3.   Cover pressure cooker and bring up to full pressure (15 pounds). Reduce heat to stabilize pressure and cook for 12 minutes. Release pressure. Stir in the sour cream and caraway. Serve hot, topped with additional sour cream, if desired. The goulash can be made in advance and refrigerated or frozen.

WINTER BEEF AND VEGETABLE STEW

This is an old family favorite that deviates from the original recipe only when it comes to cooking. Stovetop simmering—a 2½-hour labor of love—gives way to one-fifth the time when the pressure cooker is called into action. The result is stew as it is meant to be—a richly flavored amalgam of tender meat and vibrantly fresh vegetables in a richly flavored sauce.

Preparation time: 15 minutes
Pressure cooking time: 22 minutes
Other cooking time: 10 minutes

Yield: 4 servings

2 tablespoons flour
Salt and freshly ground black pepper to taste
1½ pounds beef stew meat such as chuck, cubed
2 tablespoons vegetable oil
2 tablespoons red wine vinegar
1 medium onion, about 5 ounces, diced
1 cup chicken stock or broth
2 tablespoons tomato paste
½ teaspoon dried basil
3 medium carrots
2 small stalks celery
1 large potato
1 cup tiny frozen peas, thawed
1 teaspoon Worcestershire sauce
1 teaspoon Dijon mustard

1.   Combine the flour and salt and pepper to taste in a large paper bag. Add meat and shake until well coated with flour. Heat 1 tablespoon oil in the pressure cooker. Add half of the meat and cook over high heat until browned. Remove and set aside. Heat remaining oil and brown the rest of the meat. Set aside.

2.   Add the vinegar to the pan and stir up the browned bits from the bottom of the pan. Add the onion and cook 2 minutes, stirring often. Add the meat, chicken stock or broth, tomato paste, and basil. Cover pressure cooker and bring up to full pressure (15 pounds). Reduce heat to stabilize pressure and cook for 15 minutes.

3.   Meanwhile, prepare the other vegetables. Peel the carrots. Cut the carrots and celery into ½-inch slices. Cut the unpeeled potato into 1-inch cubes.

4.   After the stew has cooked 15 minutes, release pressure and add the carrots, celery, and potato. Cover pressure cooker and bring up to full pressure (15 pounds). Reduce heat to stabilize pressure and cook for 7 minutes. Release pressure immediately and stir in the peas, Worcestershire sauce, and mustard. The stew can be made in advance and refrigerated or frozen. Reheat on the stove or in the microwave oven.

CURRIED BEEF

The exotic combination of spices gives this stew a rich flavor and aroma that belies the quick cooking. It's not a hot curry, but rather one that takes its character from the fragrant mix of spices. The amount of cayenne pepper given here makes a very tame dish. Add more as you please. Pork or lamb can be used in place of the beef.

Traditionally, curried dishes are served with an array of colorful garnishes, anything from raisins to peanuts to cucumbers in yogurt. For a simple meal, just add rice and chutney.

Preparation time: 10 minutes
Pressure cooking time: 20 minutes
Other cooking time: 3 minutes

Yield: 4 to 6 servings

½ teaspoon ground coriander
½ teaspoon paprika
½ teaspoon turmeric
⅛ teaspoon cayenne pepper, or to taste
⅛ teaspoon ground clove
⅛ teaspoon ground cinnamon
⅛ teaspoon ground cardamom
1 bay leaf
1 teaspoon ground cumin
Salt to taste
1 large clove garlic
1 piece fresh ginger, about ¾-inch cube
2 medium onions, about 8 ounces total
3 tablespoons unsalted butter
2 pounds beef round, cut into large cubes
⅓ cup plus 1 tablespoon water
2 tablespoons tomato paste
2 teaspoons red wine vinegar
1½ tablespoons flour

1.   Combine coriander, paprika, turmeric, cayenne pepper, clove, cinnamon, cardamom, bay leaf, cumin, and salt to taste in a small dish and set aside. Mince the garlic and ginger. Cut the onions into ½-inch cubes.

2.   Melt the butter in the pressure cooker. Stir in the spice mixture, garlic, and ginger and cook 1 minute. Add the onions and cook 1 minute longer. Add the meat, $\frac{1}{3}$ cup water, and tomato paste. Cover pressure cooker and bring up to full pressure (15 pounds). Reduce heat to stabilize pressure and cook for 20 minutes. Release pressure.

3.   Combine the remaining 1 tablespoon water and the vinegar with the flour to make a smooth paste. Stir in several tablespoons of the broth from the meat, then stir the flour mixture back into the meat broth. Cook over high heat until thickened, 1 to 2 minutes. The curry can be refrigerated for up to 4 days or frozen.

BEEF STROGANOFF

Rich and amply endowed with tender strips of beef and mushrooms, this classic dish is a natural for cooking in the pressure cooker. Sour cream is not altogether authentic but is favored by most people. It smooths out the dish and gives it a wonderfully creamy finish.

Preparation time: 15 minutes
Pressure cooking time: 10 minutes
Other cooking time: 8 minutes

Yield: 4 servings

½ pound mushrooms
2 small onions
1¼ pounds lean beef sirloin
1 medium tomato
3 tablespoons unsalted butter
Salt and freshly ground black pepper to taste
2 tablespoons flour
½ cup beef stock or broth
1 teaspoon Worcestershire sauce
¼ cup sour cream

1.   Cut the mushrooms into thick slices. Slice the onions. Cut the beef into strips about ½ inch thick by 2½ inches long. Peel and seed the tomato and dice.

2.   Melt 2 tablespoons butter in the pressure cooker. Add the mushrooms and onions, and cook over medium-high heat until tender. Set aside. Melt the remaining butter in the pressure cooker. Add the meat and brown well on all sides. Season with salt and pepper to taste, then sprinkle the flour over the top. Add the stock or broth and Worcestershire sauce.

3.   Cover pressure cooker and bring up to full pressure (15 pounds). Reduce heat to stabilize pressure and cook for 10 minutes. Release pressure and add the mushrooms, onions, tomato, and sour cream. Stir gently and heat, if necessary, but do not let it come to a boil.

MEXICAN MEATBALL STEW WITH VEGETABLES

Olé!—meatballs cooked in just 10 minutes, with a colorful crop of fresh vegetables to boot. The meatballs are made from ground turkey instead of beef or pork, so they're extra lean. And in keeping with the lighter stance, no fat is added. Serve with rice or cornbread.

Preparation time: 20 minutes
Pressure cooking time: 10 minutes

Yield: 3 to 4 servings

1 slice soft white bread
3 tablespoons milk
2 tablespoons finely diced onion
¾ teaspoon cumin seeds
¼ teaspoon salt
1 pound ground turkey
2 tablespoons flour, plus more if needed
¼ cup chicken stock or broth
1 14½-ounce can tomatoes, chopped coarse
½ teaspoon chili powder
2 large carrots
2 medium stalks celery
1 ear sweet corn
Fresh minced cilantro, if desired

1. Break the bread into small pieces and put in a mixing bowl with the milk, onion, ¼ teaspoon cumin seeds, and salt. Let stand 5 minutes. Stir with a spoon to break up the bread as much as possible. Add the turkey and mix well.

2. Shape the meat mixture into eight equal-sized meatballs, flouring your hands if the meat is too soft to handle easily.

3. Stir the chicken stock or broth and 2 tablespoons flour together to make a smooth paste. Add to pressure cooker along with tomatoes, chili powder, and remaining ½ teaspoon cumin seeds.

4. Peel carrots and cut in half crosswise. Cut each half lengthwise into quarters. Bias-cut each celery stalk into four pieces. Cut

the corn into four pieces. Add the vegetables and meatballs to pressure cooker.

5.   Cover pressure cooker and bring up to full pressure (15 pounds). Reduce heat to stabilize pressure and cook for 10 minutes. Release pressure. Add cilantro, if desired.

VEAL RAGOUT WITH DILLED CARROTS

The mild flavor of veal is well enhanced by a bounty of sweet, colorful carrots and the sprightly taste of dill. Serve with rice or buttered noodles.

Preparation time: 10 minutes
Pressure cooking time: 15 minutes
Other cooking time: 5 minutes

Yield: 4 servings

2 tablespoons flour
Salt and freshly ground black pepper to taste
1½ pounds lean veal stew meat
2 teaspoons unsalted butter
2 teaspoons vegetable oil
1 medium onion, about 5 ounces
4 large carrots, about 12 ounces
½ cup chicken stock or broth
1 tablespoon Dijon mustard
⅓ cup whipping cream or half-and-half
1½ teaspoons dried dill weed

1.   Combine the flour and salt and pepper to taste in a large plastic food bag. Add the veal and shake the bag so the veal is coated with flour. Heat the butter and oil in the pressure cooker. Add the veal and brown well.

2.   Dice the onion. Cut the carrots into ¾-inch-thick slices. Add the onion and carrots to the meat and cook 1 minute. Add the stock or broth and mustard. Cover pressure cooker and bring up to full pressure (15 pounds). Reduce heat to stabilize pressure and cook for 15 minutes.

3.   Release pressure, stir in the cream and dill, and adjust seasoning.

LAMB AND FETA STUFFED PEPPERS

That stuffed peppers cook in such a short amount of time is something you have to try to believe. Four minutes is right, not 14 or 24. Even the initial step of blanching the pepper is eliminated, a boon to cooks in a hurry. The peppers cook right along with the filling, emerging from the cooker soft and tender. The filling is enlivened with feta cheese and seasoned with traditional Greek herbs. Orzo, a tiny pasta that looks like rice, is available in more and more supermarkets now. It's a nice change from rice, but certainly rice is good, too.

If the price of yellow, orange, and red peppers isn't prohibitive, use one of each in addition to one green.

Preparation time: 10 minutes
Pressure cooking time: 4 minutes
Other cooking time: 5 minutes

Yield: 4 servings

4 large bell peppers
4 green onions
1 medium clove garlic
1 pound ground lamb
1 cup cooked orzo or rice
⅓ cup tomato sauce or prepared meatless spaghetti sauce
½ teaspoon dried mint
½ teaspoon dried oregano
Salt and freshly ground black pepper to taste
4 ounces feta cheese, diced
1 cup water

1.   Cut the tops from the peppers and remove the seeds and membranes. Set the peppers aside. Dice the tops of the peppers to equal ¼ cup. Slice the green onions and mince the garlic.

2.   Brown the lamb in the pressure cooker. Pour off any fat and add the chopped pepper tops, green onions, and garlic. Cook 1 minute.

3.   Transfer meat mixture to a bowl and add the cooked orzo, tomato sauce, mint, oregano, and salt and pepper to taste and mix well. Gently fold in the feta. Divide the filling among the 4 peppers.

4.   Put 1 cup of water in the bottom of the pressure cooker and put the trivet in place. Stand the peppers on the trivet. Cover pressure cooker and bring up to full pressure (15 pounds). Reduce heat to stabilize pressure and cook for 4 minutes. Release pressure and serve immediately.

GREEN CHILE PORK AND HOMINY STEW

Southwestern tastes abound in this lively stew. Big chunks of pork, cooked until they are meltingly tender, are joined by diced poblano peppers, tomatillos, hominy, and a generous handful of minced cilantro.

Preparation time: 15 minutes
Pressure cooking time: 22 minutes
Other cooking time: 10 minutes

Yield: 6 servings

2 tablespoons vegetable oil
1 teaspoon cumin seeds
¼ cup flour
1 tablespoon light brown sugar
1 teaspoon dried oregano
Salt and freshly ground black pepper to taste
2 pounds cubed pork stew meat
1 small onion, about 3 ounces
1 large clove garlic
1 serrano or jalapeño pepper
1 tablespoon sherry wine vinegar or red wine vinegar
1¼ cups chicken stock or broth
3 poblano peppers
4 tomatillos
1 15-ounce can hominy, drained and rinsed
1 cup fresh cilantro leaves, minced

1.   Heat 1 tablespoon oil in the pressure cooker. Add the cumin seeds and cook over medium-low heat until they are fragrant, 2 to 3 minutes. Remove from heat and set aside.

2.   Combine the flour, brown sugar, oregano, and salt and pepper to taste in a large plastic food bag. Add the meat and shake the bag to coat the meat with the flour. Add half of the meat to the pressure cooker and brown well over medium-high heat. Remove with a slotted spoon and set aside. Heat the remaining tablespoon oil and brown the other half of the meat. Set aside.

3.   Mince the onion, garlic, and serrano pepper. Add to the pan and cook until they just begin to soften, about 2 minutes. Add the vinegar and stir up any browned bits from the bottom of the pan. Add the stock or broth and return the meat to the pressure cooker.

4.   Cover pressure cooker and bring up to full pressure (15 pounds). Reduce heat to stabilize pressure and cook for 20 minutes.

5.   While the pork is cooking, seed the poblanos and cut into squares. Dice the tomatillos. After the pork has cooked for 20 minutes, release pressure and add the poblano peppers, tomatillos, and hominy. Cover pressure cooker and bring up to full pressure (15 pounds). Reduce heat to stabilize pressure and cook for 2 minutes. Release pressure and stir in the cilantro. Adjust the seasoning with additional salt and pepper to taste.

SPANISH PAELLA

The lengthy ingredients list and number of steps in this recipe may seem imposing, but the work is all very simple and results in a very pretty and festive party dish. In Spain, paella is traditionally served with a bounty of fresh seafood.

Although it is an important component in the dish, saffron adds considerably to the cost. Ground turmeric can be used in its place, which will give the dish its characteristic golden color though not its flavor.

Preparation time: 30 minutes plus 30 minutes standing time
Pressure cooking time: 9 minutes
Other cooking time: 15 minutes

Yield: 4 servings

1 medium clove garlic
1 tablespoon sherry vinegar or red wine vinegar
¼ teaspoon ground coriander
¼ teaspoon paprika
Salt and freshly ground black pepper
4 chicken thighs, skin removed
1 large red bell pepper
½ pound Spanish chorizo
1 large tomato, about 8 ounces
1 large onion, about 8 ounces
1 tablespoon olive oil
1¼ cups long grain rice
¼ cup dry white wine
2 cups chicken stock or broth
½ teaspoon saffron threads, or ½ teaspoon ground turmeric
½ teaspoon dried marjoram
1 cup frozen tiny peas, thawed

1.   Mince the garlic. Place it in a large plastic food bag along with vinegar, coriander, paprika, ¼ teaspoon salt, and pepper to taste. Add the chicken thighs. Working through the bag, rub the seasoning mixture into the chicken. Set aside for 30 minutes.

2.   Meanwhile, roast the red pepper either by placing it directly over an open flame and turning it until the skin is completely blackened or by cutting off 4 flat sides, arranging them on a baking sheet and broiling, close to the heat, until blackened. Either way,

put the pepper in a paper bag until it is cool enough to handle. Then peel away the blackened skin, rinsing under cold water if necessary to help remove it. Cut the pepper into ½-inch cubes and set aside.

3.　Cut the chorizo into ½-inch-thick slices. Cut the tomato in half crosswise and squeeze gently to remove the seeds. Dice the tomato and onion.

4.　Heat the oil in the pressure cooker. Add the chorizo and cook until well browned. Remove the chorizo with a slotted spoon and set aside. Add the chicken, meaty-side down. Cook, turning once, until well browned. Set chicken aside and pour off all but 2 tablespoons fat from the pan. Add the onion to the pan and cook, stirring constantly, until softened, about 3 minutes.

5.　Add the rice to the onion and stir so it is coated with oil. Pour in the wine and use a wooden spoon to scrape up any browned bits from the bottom of the pan. Cook until the wine has evaporated. Add the chicken stock or broth, tomato, saffron or turmeric, marjoram, and salt and pepper to taste and stir well. Return the chicken to the pan, pressing it slightly into the liquid.

6.　Cover pressure cooker and bring up to full pressure (15 pounds). Reduce heat to stabilize pressure and cook for 9 minutes. Release pressure and add the chorizo, roasted pepper, and peas. Cook, uncovered, until they are just heated through.

Note: Spanish chorizo is a link sausage that is much firmer than its Mexican counterpart. It is less commonly available than Mexican chorizo. If it is not available, use another smoked link sausage such as andouille or kielbasa. Mexican chorizo will crumble too much. If the sausage you use is not spicy, add a small minced hot pepper or cayenne pepper to taste. The paella should have a very slight bite to it.

Note: If you wish to add seafood, cook 16 medium shrimp in a small amount of boiling salted water until they turn pink. Do not overcook them. Remove the beards from 12 mussels and soak the mussels in cold water for 20 minutes. Discard any mussels that are open. Drain well. Scrub 4 clams. Heat the mussels and clams in a covered pan, just until the shells open. Keep warm. Stir the shrimp into the finished paella and use the clams and mussels as a border around the edge of the serving dish.

JAMBALAYA

Jambalaya is a wonderful jumble of ingredients—meat, sausage, and seafood cooked together with tomatoey rice and Cajun seasonings. In the pressure cooker, it develops the same full, rich taste as the slow-cooked version, but in just a few short minutes. Though it is certainly easy and quick enough to make for after-work dinners, jambalaya is special enough for entertaining.

Preparation time: 15 minutes
Pressure cooking time: 8 minutes
Other cooking time: 10 minutes

Yield: 5 cups, 4 servings

1 large onion, about 8 ounces
1 large green bell pepper, 7 to 8 ounces
3 medium stalks celery, about 6 ounces total
1 large clove garlic
6 ounces smoked sausage, such as andouille or kielbasa
1 whole boneless chicken breast
1 tablespoon vegetable oil
6 ounces medium shell-on shrimp
1 cup converted long grain rice
1½ cups chicken stock or broth
1 cup tomato sauce with tomato bits
1 bay leaf
½ teaspoon dried thyme
¼ teaspoon cayenne pepper or to taste
3 to 4 dashes red pepper sauce
Salt and freshly ground black pepper to taste

1.   Dice the onion. Cut the green pepper into 1-inch squares. Cut the celery into ¼-inch slices. Mince the garlic. Cut the sausage into ¼-inch-thick slices. Cut the chicken into bite-sized chunks.

2.   Heat the oil in the pressure cooker. Add the sausage, chicken, and shrimp and cook over medium-high heat, stirring often, until the chicken and shrimp are firm and cooked through, about 4 minutes. Do not overcook. Remove from the pan and set aside. Set the shrimp aside and peel them when they are cool enough to handle.

3.   Add the onion, green pepper, celery, and garlic to the pressure cooker and cook, stirring often, until the vegetables begin to soften, 3 to 4 minutes. Stir in the rice and cook 1 minute longer. Add the stock or broth, tomato sauce, bay leaf, thyme, cayenne pepper, red pepper sauce, and salt and black pepper to taste.

4.   Cover pressure cooker and bring up to full pressure (15 pounds). Reduce heat to stabilize pressure and cook for 8 minutes. Release pressure and remove cover. Stir in sausage, chicken, and shrimp, cover pressure cooker, and let stand for 5 minutes. Adjust the seasoning and serve hot. The jambalaya can be refrigerated for up to 3 days. Reheat on the stove or in the microwave oven, adding additional stock or tomato juice if it is too dry.

6
FISH AND SEAFOOD

TUNA NICOISE

TAHITIAN SWORDFISH

SALMON "TAMALES"

POACHED HALIBUT WITH GRIBICHE SAUCE

FISHERMAN'S WHARF CIOPPINO

PAN-ASIAN SHRIMP WITH PEPPERS

STEAMED MUSSELS WITH
THAI-FLAVORED BUTTER

By its very nature, fish cookery is quick. For simple preparation, no fish takes more than a matter of minutes to prepare, whether it's a fillet or steak or whether it's boiled, poached, steamed, or sautéed. The conventional wisdom is that since fish cooks so quickly, there is no advantage to using the pressure cooker. I was tempted to be swept along by that notion myself. Curiosity got the better of me, though, and one day, as I prepared to poach some halibut, I thought, "Why a sauté pan and not a pressure cooker?" Needless to say, the halibut landed in the pressure cooker, and I was hooked.

For a certain style of fish preparation, the pressure cooker easily rivals other methods of preparation in both ease and results. Providing it's not overdone, fish prepared in the pressure cooker is tender and juicy and has the benefit of being cooked right along with some wonderful flavoring ingredients. Any juices from the fish are captured in the sauce or the poaching liquid, so none of the sea-sweet flavor gets away.

No matter what method you use to cook fish, the difference between perfectly cooked and hopelessly overcooked is measured in mere seconds, not minutes. When preparing fish in the pressure cooker, be especially mindful of the timer. Don't leave the kitchen once the fish starts to cook, since it will be done in practically no time at all. The timing is always variable, depending on the thickness of the fish. I have given cooking times that are at the low end so the fish doesn't end up overcooked, which is, sadly, irreversible. If it is not done to your liking, simply replace the cover and cook a bit longer.

When using the pressure cooker for fish, avoid those varieties that are thin and delicate, such as sole, cod, pike, and whitefish. Focus instead on meatier species of fish and the results will be uniformly successful, not to mention quick.

Though it's often stated, the caveat bears repeating: Make sure the fish you buy is as fresh as can be. If it doesn't look and smell as though it was swimming until quite recently, pass on it until the selection is better.

TUNA NICOISE

The lusty flavors of southern France go well with the "meaty" taste and texture of fresh tuna. Swordfish can be prepared the same way.

Preparation time: 10 minutes
Pressure cooking time: 3½ to 4 minutes
Other cooking time: 3 minutes

Yield: 2 servings

1 large clove garlic
1 large shallot
2 small ripe tomatoes, about 8 ounces total
1½ tablespoons olive oil
¼ cup dry white wine or vermouth
⅛ teaspoon dried red pepper flakes, or more to taste
Salt and freshly ground black pepper to taste
2 tuna steaks, about 6 to 7 ounces, cut about ½ inch thick
8 oil-cured black olives
2 tablespoons julienned fresh basil, or ½ teaspoon dried

1.　Mince the garlic and shallot. Core the tomatoes, cut in half crosswise, and squeeze gently to remove the seeds. Dice the tomatoes.

2.　Heat the oil in the pressure cooker. Add the garlic and shallots and cook over medium heat until softened, about 2 minutes. Add the tomatoes and cook 1 minute longer. Add the wine, red pepper flakes, and salt and pepper to taste. If you are using dried basil, add it now. Place the tuna on top and spoon some of the tomato mixture over the fish.

3.　Cover pressure cooker and place over high heat. **Start timing immediately** and cook for 3½ minutes for fish that is still slightly pink in the center, or longer as desired. Release pressure immediately. Add the olives and fresh basil, if used, and adjust the seasoning. Serve the fish with the tomato mixture spooned over the top.

TAHITIAN SWORDFISH

The cool, refreshing flavor of fresh ginger and the tang of citrus, set off with the slightest bite from dried peppers, lend a tropical taste to these swordfish steaks.

Preparation time: 10 minutes plus 4 hours marinating time
Pressure cooking time: 3 minutes

Yield: 4 servings

¾ cup fresh cilantro
2 small cloves garlic
1 piece fresh ginger, about ¾-inch cube
2 strips orange zest
2 strips lime zest
⅓ cup vegetable oil
4½ tablespoons seasoned rice vinegar (or rice vinegar mixed with
*   sugar to taste)*
2 tablespoons orange juice
¼ teaspoon crushed red pepper flakes
Salt to taste
4 swordfish steaks, about ½ inch thick
Fresh cilantro sprigs for garnish

1.   Mince the cilantro, garlic, ginger, orange zest, and lime zest in a food processor or by hand. Mix with the oil, vinegar, orange juice, red pepper flakes, and salt to taste. Transfer to a large plastic food bag and add the swordfish. Seal the bag and turn it over several times so the fish is well coated. Refrigerate at least 4 hours or overnight.

2.   Transfer the fish and marinade to the pressure cooker. Cover pressure cooker and bring up to full pressure (15 pounds). Reduce heat to stabilize pressure and cook for 3 minutes. Release pressure immediately. The fish should be firm but not hard. Add more time if necessary, taking care not to overcook the fish. Spoon the marinade over the fish and garnish with sprigs of cilantro.

SALMON "TAMALES"

Big nuggets of salmon, mixed with a colorful assortment of vegetables, nestle in corn husks for a "nouveau" version of tamales. They're easy to put together yet make a dramatic and whimsically fun presentation. The butter enriches the salmon but can be left out for a rendition that is lower in fat but still quite delicious.

Preparation time: 10 minutes plus 20 minutes soaking time
Pressure cooking time: 4 minutes

Yield: 2 servings

6 dried corn husks for tamales
Hot water
2 large salmon steaks, about 1 pound total
¼ cup finely diced red or orange bell pepper
¼ cup fresh or frozen thawed sweet corn
3 tablespoons coarsely chopped cilantro
2 small green onions, cut in rings
½ teaspoon finely minced seeded hot pepper, or more to taste
1½ tablespoons unsalted butter, melted, if desired
1 tablespoon seasoned rice vinegar
½ teaspoon Dijon mustard
⅛ teaspoon ground cumin
Salt to taste

1.   Put the corn husks in a large shallow dish and cover completely with hot water. Let stand 20 minutes to soften.

2.   Meanwhile, remove the skin and bones from the salmon and cut the fish into large, bite-sized chunks. Transfer to a mixing bowl and add the bell pepper, corn, cilantro, green onions, hot pepper, butter, vinegar, mustard, cumin, and salt to taste. Toss gently. Let stand 10 minutes or until the corn husks are softened.

3.   Pat the husks dry. Put half of the salmon mixture into one of the husks, leaving about 1½ inches of space on each end. Top with another husk, placing it so the filling is completely enclosed. Use a third husk if necessary to cover the filling. Fill the other tamale the same way. Twist the ends to seal them and secure with kitchen twine.

4.   Put 1 cup water into the bottom of the pressure cooker and put

the trivet in place. Bring the water to a boil, then add the filled husks. Cover pressure cooker and bring up to full pressure (15 pounds). Reduce heat to stabilize pressure and cook for 4 minutes. Reduce pressure immediately.

Note: Dried corn husks are available in many Latin American groceries and some large supermarkets. Fresh corn husks can be used in their place. If you are using fresh husks, select the largest outer leaves. It is not necessary to soak the fresh husks.

POACHED HALIBUT WITH GRIBICHE SAUCE

Many varieties of fish, including halibut, are well suited to poaching in this aromatic liquid. The sauce, a French classic, offers a tart contrast to the sweet-flavored halibut. It goes well on monkfish and sea bass as well. If you like a lot of sauce on your fish, you might want to double the sauce ingredients.

Preparation time: 15 minutes
Pressure cooking time: 3½ minutes

Yield: 4 servings

Sauce

2 tablespoons red wine vinegar
1 tablespoon fresh lemon juice
½ teaspoon Dijon mustard
5 tablespoons oil, preferably a mix of olive oil and vegetable oil
2 tablespoons minced sweet red or white onion
2 teaspoons finely minced cornichon pickles
1 teaspoon drained capers
Salt and freshly ground black pepper to taste

Poaching Liquid

1 cup water
¼ cup dry white wine or dry vermouth
2 teaspoons white wine vinegar
2 bay leaves
2 sprigs fresh herbs, such as parsley, basil, or thyme
2 slices onion, separated into rings
2 whole peppercorns
4 halibut fillets, about 6 ounces each

1.   For the sauce, combine the vinegar, lemon juice, and mustard in a bowl. Slowly whisk in the oil, mixing until slightly thickened. Add the remaining sauce ingredients and set aside.

2.   For the poaching liquid, combine all the ingredients in the pressure cooker. Add the halibut skin-side up. Cover and lock pressure cooker and place over high heat. **Start timing immediately** and cook for 3½ minutes. Release the pressure immediately. The fish should be firm and opaque. If it needs more cooking, replace the cover and cook briefly.

3.   Transfer the fish to warm serving plates, using a slotted spatula and letting it drain well. Spoon the sauce over the fish and serve immediately.

FISHERMAN'S WHARF CIOPPINO

There are many regional American fish soups, clam chowder being popular on the East Coast, cioppino in the western environs. This version of cioppino uses fish and shellfish that are readily available almost everywhere, but feel free to explore the local resources and use whatever is at hand.

Preparation time: 15 minutes
Pressure cooking time: 5 minutes
Other cooking time: 5 minutes

Yield: 4 main course servings

12 mussels
2 large cloves garlic
1 medium onion, 5 to 6 ounces
1 large stalk celery
2 tablespoons olive oil
1 cup dry white wine
3 medium tomatoes, peeled and seeded
1 15- or 16-ounce can tomato sauce
1 8-ounce bottle clam juice
$\frac{1}{2}$ teaspoon dried thyme
$\frac{1}{2}$ teaspoon dried marjoram
$\frac{1}{2}$ teaspoon sugar
$\frac{1}{4}$ teaspoon crushed red pepper flakes
8 ounces firm-fleshed fish, such as red snapper, cut in
* $1\frac{1}{4}$-inch chunks*
4 ounces bay scallops
12 large shrimp, peeled
1 small red pepper, diced fine
$\frac{1}{2}$ cup minced fresh herbs, such as parsley, cilantro, or basil
Salt and freshly ground black pepper to taste

1.   Pull the beards from the mussels. Put the mussels in a bowl of cold salted water to soak while you proceed with the soup. Discard any mussels that open during soaking.

2.   Mince the garlic and onion. Dice the celery. Heat the oil in the pressure cooker. Add the garlic, onion, and celery and cook until they begin to soften, 3 to 4 minutes. Add the wine and boil over high heat 1 minute.

3.   Dice the tomatoes and add them to the pan along with tomato sauce, clam juice, thyme, marjoram, sugar, and red pepper flakes. Cover pressure cooker and bring up to full pressure (15 pounds). Reduce heat to stabilize pressure and cook for 5 minutes.

4.   Release pressure. Drain the mussels well and add them to the pressure cooker along with the fish, scallops, shrimp, and red pepper. Cover and lock the pressure cooker and bring up to 5 pounds pressure. Release pressure as soon as 5 pounds pressure is reached. The mussels should be open and the fish should be opaque. Stir in the minced herbs and season with salt and pepper to taste.

PAN-ASIAN SHRIMP WITH PEPPERS

Little bits of red and yellow bell peppers, pink-tinted shrimp, and snippets of fresh herbs make this a lively, colorful dish full of fresh flavors. A bit of hot pepper adds a spicy bite, which is offset by the sweet flavor of the rice vinegar and the cooling effects of fresh mint. Serve over cooked rice or angel hair pasta.

Preparation time: 10 minutes
Pressure cooking time: 1 minute
Other cooking time: 5 minutes

Yield: 3 to 4 servings

1 medium onion, about 4 ounces
1 tablespoon vegetable oil
½ teaspoon Oriental sesame oil
1 medium red bell pepper
1 medium yellow bell pepper
1 small jalapeño or serrano pepper, seeded if desired
1 small piece fresh ginger, about the size of a quarter
¼ cup chicken stock or broth
3 tablespoons seasoned rice vinegar
3 tablespoons dry sherry
½ teaspoon sugar
1 pound large, peeled shrimp
1½ teaspoons cornstarch mixed with 1½ teaspoons water
2 tablespoons minced fresh mint leaves
2 tablespoons minced fresh cilantro

1.   Dice the onion. Heat both oils in the pressure cooker. Add the onion and cook over medium heat until softened, 3 to 4 minutes.

2.   Dice the red and yellow bell peppers. Mince the jalapeño pepper and ginger. Add these ingredients to the pressure cooker along with the stock or broth, vinegar, sherry, and sugar and mix well. Add the shrimp.

3.   Cover pressure cooker and bring up to full pressure (15 pounds). Reduce heat to stabilize pressure and cook for 1 minute. Release pressure immediately and stir in the cornstarch mixture. Cook, uncovered, over medium heat until the sauce thickens slightly, about 30 seconds. Remove from heat and add the mint and cilantro.

STEAMED MUSSELS WITH
THAI-FLAVORED BUTTER

Cooking mussels is never a lengthy proposition, whether the job is done in a pot, a microwave oven, or a pressure cooker. The pressure cooker, however, offers one big advantage. Because the mussels are cooked in a tightly sealed pot, their strong aroma doesn't travel the length of the house. After they've cooked, reduce the pressure by holding the cooker under cold running water and there will be practically no cooking odor.

Larger and meatier green-lipped mussels from New Zealand are becoming more common in fish markets. Try them if they're available. Their shells are very pretty—variegated brown that turns to a vibrant green at the edge—and the bright orange meat is mild and delicious.

Preparation time: 10 minutes plus 30 minutes soaking time
Pressure cooking time: 3½ minutes
Other cooking time: 5 minutes

Yield: 4 servings as a first course, 2 as a main dish

2 pounds mussels
Cold, salted water
2 stalks lemongrass
1 small hot pepper
4 tablespoons unsalted butter
2 tablespoons seasoned rice vinegar
1 tablespoon fresh lime juice
2 tablespoons coconut milk or whipping cream
3 tablespoons minced fresh herbs, either cilantro or a mix of
*   cilantro, mint, and basil*
1 cup water

1.   Pull the beards from the mussels. Put the mussels in a large bowl and cover with cold salted water. Let stand 30 minutes. If any open after soaking, discard them.

2.   While the mussels are soaking, trim the long dried ends and one or two dried outer layers of the lemongrass. Mince the soft white core (about 2½ to 3 inches). Mince the hot pepper, using as

many of the hotter seeds as desired. The dish should be mildly spicy but not overpoweringly hot.

3.   Melt the butter in the pressure cooker. Add the lemongrass, hot pepper, vinegar, and lime juice. Cook gently for 5 minutes, then strain, add the coconut milk or cream and the herbs, and set aside.

4.   Put 1 cup water in the bottom of the pressure cooker. Add the trivet and put the cleaned mussels on the trivet. Close the pressure cooker and put over high heat. **Start timing immediately** and cook for 3½ minutes. Run cold water over the top of the pressure cooker to reduce the pressure. Open the cooker. All the mussels should be opened. If not, transfer those that are fully opened to large, shallow soup dishes. Cover the pressure cooker and cook another 30 to 60 seconds or until all the mussels have opened. Pour the butter mixture over the mussels and serve immediately.

Note: Fresh lemongrass is available in Thai markets and some large supermarkets.

7
VEGETABLES

■

RATATOUILLE NICOISE

CURRIED POTATOES AND PEAS

CIAMBOTTA

SPAGHETTI SQUASH WITH PESTO

EGGPLANT WITH MOZZARELLA AND TOMATOES

ZUCCHINI STUFFED WITH
COUSCOUS AND VEGETABLES

SHRIMP-STUFFED ARTICHOKES

Vegetables cook extremely well in the pressure cooker. Their color, texture, and marvelous good taste are all left in their glory by this quick method and, since they haven't been assaulted by lengthy cooking, much of their vitamin and mineral content remains intact. Pressure steaming is the method of choice for simple vegetable preparations.

To pressure steam vegetables, add 1 cup water to the pressure cooker. Keep in mind that uniformly sized vegetables will cook more evenly. Place the vegetables in the steamer basket, cover, and bring up to full pressure (15 pounds). Once full pressure is reached, begin timing.

After the allotted cooking time, release the pressure quickly by holding the cooker under cold running water. This prevents the vegetables from becoming overcooked since seconds, not to mention minutes, can make a tremendous difference. If the vegetables aren't fully cooked to your liking, replace and lock the cover and cook longer.

The vegetable cooking chart that follows covers almost any vegetable you'll ever consider popping into the pressure cooker. The cooking times given are for what is usually described as al dente vegetables—those that are tender but still crisp. If you wish to puree vegetables, increase their cooking time by 50 percent to 100 percent (for purees, the vegetables should be extremely tender when pierced with a knife). For those vegetables that have cooking times listed as 0 to ½ minutes, remove the cooker from the heat as soon as full pressure is reached, and release the pressure.

These cooking times are meant to be guidelines at best, which can be altered to fit circumstances and taste. Experience, which comes quickly, will ultimately be your best guide. Unless you're the type of person who can't bear to write in cookbooks, you may want to make notes that reflect your own preferences right on the cooking chart.

FRESH VEGETABLE COOKING TIMES

Vegetable	Minutes after High Pressure Reached
Artichokes: whole, 10 to 12 ounces	9 to 11
Asparagus: 15 to 20 to the pound, stems peeled	0 to ½
Beans, green: whole, slender	0 to ½
Beets: whole, unpeeled, about 2½ inches in diameter	12 to 15
peeled, ¼-inch-thick slices	1½ to 2
Broccoli: stems peeled and cut into spears, medium flowerettes	1½ to 2
Brussels sprouts: medium-sized, about 1¼ inches in diameter	2 to 3
Cabbage: wedges	5 to 7
1-inch shreds	1 to 2

Vegetable	Minutes after High Pressure Reached
Carrots: ¼-inch slices	1½ to 2
1-inch chunks	4 to 6
Cauliflower: 1¼-inch flowerettes	1 to 2
Chayote squash: 1-inch chunks	1 to 2
Corn: tender ears, sweet corn	2 to 3
Eggplant: 1-inch cubes or slices	1 to 2
Kohlrabi: ¼-inch slices or ¼-inch juliennes	1 to 2
Okra: medium-sized pods, about 4 inches	1 to 2
Pearl onions: about 1¼ inches, peeled after cooking	4 to 6
Parsnips: medium, split in half lengthwise, halved crosswise	2 to 3
Potatoes: peeled and cut into 2-inch cubes	5 to 7
Tiny new potatoes: about 1½ inches in diameter	3 to 6
Rutabaga (Swedes): cut into 1-inch cubes	5 to 8
Squash, hard winter: peeled, cut into 1-inch cubes	4 to 7
Squash, acorn: about 1½ pounds, halved	10 to 14
Squash, spaghetti: about 2¼ pounds, halved	13 to 17
Squash, zucchini or summer: ¾-inch slices, halved if large	0 to ½
Sweet potatoes: whole, about 8 ounces each	7 to 11
Turnips: ¼-inch-thick slices	½ to 1
Small whole, about 2 inches in diameter	8 to 12

RATATOUILLE NICOISE

Originally hailing from Provence, France, ratatouille has become pretty familiar to most Americans, with good reason. If there is a more felicitous pairing of vegetables, I haven't found it. Ratatouille can be served hot or at room temperature, folded into an omelette or tossed into a tangle of pasta, eaten plain or embellished with some cheese and a poached egg. Use several colors of bell peppers if you can. Red, yellow, and orange give the dish stand-out good looks.

Salting and draining zucchini and eggplant removes much of their liquid, which can be bitter. Some cooks opt to skip this step in the interest of saving time. When using a pressure cooker, it is essential to salt and drain these vegetables so the finished dish is not too watery.

Preparation time: 20 minutes plus 30 minutes draining time
Pressure cooking time: 4 minutes
Other cooking time: 5 minutes

Yield: 7 to 8 cups

2 medium eggplants, about 2 pounds total
5 medium zucchini, about 1¼ pounds total
Salt
2 large onions, about 1 pound total
2 large cloves garlic
1½ pounds bell peppers, preferably a mix of colors
1 pound vine-ripened summer tomatoes
¼ cup olive oil
¼ cup tomato sauce
¼ cup tomato paste
¼ cup finely slivered fresh basil, or 2 teaspoons dried
Freshly ground black pepper to taste

1.   Cut the eggplant into 1-inch cubes and the zucchini into ¼-inch-thick slices. Place eggplant and zucchini in separate colanders and toss each with about 1 teaspoon salt. Let stand 30 minutes. Wrap the eggplant in a cloth towel and squeeze firmly to remove as much moisture as possible. Set aside. Wrap and squeeze the zucchini the same way.

2.   Meanwhile, peel the onions and cut in half lengthwise. Lay them on their cut side and slice thin. Mince the garlic. Cut the bell peppers into 1-inch squares. Peel the tomatoes, if desired. Cut in half crosswise and squeeze gently to remove the seeds. Chop coarse.

3.   Heat the oil in the pressure cooker. Add the onions and garlic and cook over medium-high heat, stirring often, until they are wilted, about 5 minutes. Add the remaining vegetables, including the zucchini and eggplant, the tomato sauce, and tomato paste. If you are using dried basil, add it now as well. Stir well.

4.   Cover pressure cooker and bring up to full pressure (15 pounds). Reduce heat to stabilize pressure and cook for 4 minutes. Release pressure. Stir well and add salt and pepper to taste as well as fresh basil if used. Serve hot or at room temperature. The ratatouille can be refrigerated for up to 5 days or frozen.

CURRIED POTATOES AND PEAS

Anyone who has tasted the Indian turnovers called samosas will guess where the inspiration for this recipe came from. The same vegetables and haunting mix of spices are cooked as a vegetable side dish. The final addition of fresh herbs adds a spirited kick.

Either red or brown potatoes can be used. Brown potatoes such as Idahoes will have a dry texture, while red will be creamier.

Preparation time: 10 minutes
Pressure cooking time: 5 minutes
Other cooking time: 3 minutes

Yield: 4 to 6 servings

3 medium potatoes, about 1½ pounds total
1 small onion, about 3 ounces
1 piece fresh ginger, about ¾-inch cube
1 tablespoon unsalted butter
1 tablespoon vegetable oil
½ teaspoon cumin seeds
½ teaspoon mustard seeds
¼ teaspoon fenugreek seeds
¼ teaspoon crushed red pepper flakes
½ teaspoon turmeric
Salt to taste
1 cup chicken stock or broth, or 1 cup water
1 cup frozen peas, thawed
Minced fresh cilantro and/or fresh mint to taste

1.   Cut unpeeled potatoes into 1-inch cubes. Dice the onion and mince the ginger.

2.   Melt the butter with the oil in the pressure cooker. Add the cumin seeds, mustard seeds, fenugreek seeds, and red pepper flakes and cook over medium-high heat until they begin to darken in color and are fragrant, 2 to 3 minutes.

3.   Add the potatoes, onion, ginger, turmeric, salt to taste, and stock or broth. Cover pressure cooker and bring up to full pressure (15 pounds). Reduce heat to stabilize pressure and cook for 5 minutes. Release pressure immediately. Stir in peas. Adjust the seasoning and add the cilantro and/or mint to taste.

Note: Fenugreek seeds, small and reddish-brown, are essential to many Indian curries. They are sold at many health food stores and at Indian markets, where they are sometimes labeled as methi. In the United States, fenugreek is used as a flavoring in imitation maple syrup.

CIAMBOTTA

This Italian vegetable stew uses a harvest of fresh vegetables in a unique and versatile way. Although the ingredients are similar to those of ratatouille, the two dishes taste quite different. Ciambotta can be served as a vegetable side dish—put in a crock, covered with slices of mozzarella or provolone cheese, and broiled until the cheese is brown and bubbly—or fortified with Italian sausage for a main dish.

Preparation time: 15 minutes plus 30 minutes draining time
Pressure cooking time: 7 minutes

Yield: 5 to 6 cups

1 small eggplant, 12 to 14 ounces
Salt
1 medium onion, about 6 ounces
2 small zucchini, about 8 ounces total
1 large red potato, about 8 ounces
1 medium red or green bell pepper
3 small stalks celery, about 6 ounces total
1¼ cups prepared meatless spaghetti sauce or tomato sauce
¼ cup dry white wine
1 teaspoon dried basil
1 teaspoon dried oregano
⅛ teaspoon crushed red pepper flakes or to taste
1 tablespoon olive oil

1. If the skin on the eggplant is tough, peel eggplant. Cut into ¾-inch cubes. Place in a colander and toss lightly with about ½ teaspoon salt. Let stand 30 minutes to drain. Wrap in a cloth towel and squeeze firmly to remove as much moisture as possible.

2. Prepare the other vegetables while the eggplant is draining.

Cut the onion into wedges. Cut the zucchini, unpeeled potato, and bell pepper into ¾-inch cubes. Cut the celery on the bias into 1-inch pieces.

3.   Place all the vegetables in the pressure cooker. Add the spaghetti or tomato sauce, wine, basil, oregano, red pepper flakes, and salt to taste. Cover pressure cooker and bring up to full pressure (15 pounds). Reduce heat to stabilize pressure and cook for 7 minutes. Release pressure and stir in olive oil. Adjust the seasoning. Ciambotta can be refrigerated for up to 4 days or frozen.

SPAGHETTI SQUASH WITH PESTO

Looking at a spaghetti squash, it's not very clear why the golden, oval-shaped squash is so named. Cook it, though, and the reason becomes obvious as the inside flesh separates into a tangled mass of delicate, spaghetti-like strands. Like spaghetti, it has a mild flavor that is well enhanced by zesty flavors. Pesto sauce, an intensely flavored Italian sauce made primarily from fresh basil, is as good tossed with the squash as it is with real spaghetti. The leftover pesto can be used to give a burst of flavor to countless other recipes. Stir it into vegetable soup, add it to scrambled eggs, use it as the base for a dip or as a sensational topping for grilled lamb chops.

    Select a medium-sized squash that will fit into the pressure cooker even when cut in half. If the squash is larger, simply cook it in two batches.

Preparation time: 10 minutes
Pressure cooking time: 15 minutes

Yield: 4 servings

1 medium spaghetti squash, about 2¼ pounds
1 cup water
1 to 2 large cloves garlic
2 cups fresh basil leaves
3 ounces (¾ cup) grated Parmesan cheese
⅓ cup toasted pine nuts
Salt to taste
1 cup oil, either a mix of light olive oil and vegetable oil or all
    olive oil

1.   Carefully cut squash in half the long way. Add 1 cup water to the bottom of pressure cooker and add trivet. Place squash halves on trivet, cut-side down. Cover pressure cooker and bring up to full pressure (15 pounds). Reduce heat to stabilize pressure and cook for 15 minutes. Release pressure.

2.   Make the pesto sauce while the squash is cooking. Mince the garlic in a food processor. Add the basil, Parmesan, pine nuts, and salt to taste and process until mixture is finely ground. Add the oil and process 20 seconds.

3.   When the squash is cooked, scoop out and discard the seeds and spongy, deeper orange membrane. With a fork, rake out the strands of squash and transfer to a colander. Press lightly to remove some of the excess liquid. Transfer to a serving dish and toss with several tablespoons pesto sauce. Serve hot. Reserve the remaining pesto sauce for other uses. The sauce can be refrigerated for several weeks in a tightly covered container.

EGGPLANT WITH MOZZARELLA AND TOMATOES

The flavor of eggplant Parmesan is captured in this easily prepared and quickly cooked casserole. It makes a good meatless entree or can be served as an accompaniment to a simple meat course.

The eggplant can be cooked without the egg and bread crumb coating, though the finished dish won't be as substantial or seem as meaty. Simply brown it in the oil and skip step 2 below.

I prefer not to peel eggplant, though at times the skin is so coarse that there really isn't any choice. If the skin seems tender, leave it on. Otherwise, peel it off.

Preparation time: 15 minutes plus 30 minutes draining time
Pressure cooking time: 7 minutes
Other cooking time: 10 minutes
     Yield: 4 to 6 side dish servings, or 2 to 3 main dish servings

1 large eggplant, about 1 pound
Salt
2 large eggs, beaten
1½ cups soft bread crumbs
4 to 6 tablespoons olive oil
1 14½-ounce can stewed tomatoes
3 tablespoons minced fresh basil or 1½ teaspoons dried
1½ cups (6 ounces) shredded mozzarella cheese
¼ cup (1 ounce) minced Parmesan cheese

1.   Cut the eggplant into ¼-inch-thick round slices. Transfer to a colander, arranging the slices so the cut edges are perpendicular to the bottom of the colander. Toss with about 1 teaspoon salt, making sure to reach the cut surfaces. Let drain at least 30 minutes. Rinse and pat dry.

2.   Put the beaten eggs in a shallow dish and the bread crumbs in a pie plate. Dip the eggplant first in the egg, then in the crumbs, making sure the slices are well coated.

3.   Heat 2 tablespoons oil in the pressure cooker. Sauté the eggplant in batches until browned on both sides. Set eggplant aside as it is cooked and add more oil as necessary.

4.   Pour half of the tomatoes into the bottom of the pressure cooker and add half the eggplant, arranging it so the eggplant covers the entire bottom surface of the pan. Add half the basil and half the mozzarella cheese. Repeat the layering and sprinkle the Parmesan over all. Cover pressure cooker and bring up to full pressure (15 pounds). Reduce heat to stabilize pressure and cook for 7 minutes. Release pressure and serve hot.

ZUCCHINI STUFFED WITH COUSCOUS AND VEGETABLES

Couscous—tiny, pin-head–sized pasta—is native to Morocco, where it is often paired with colorful vegetables and bits of dried fruit. Here, just such a medley fills zucchini boats. When prepared in the pressure cooker, the couscous needs no advance cooking. It is simply stirred together with liquid and added to the hollowed-out zucchini. Then it is steamed right along with the zucchini. Serve it with simple grilled meats, especially lamb, or with chicken.

Preparation time: 15 minutes plus 30 minutes draining time
Pressure cooking time: 4 minutes
Other cooking time: 3 minutes

Yield: 4 servings

2 medium zucchini, about 8 ounces each
Salt
2 tablespoons olive oil
¼ cup pine nuts
¼ cup couscous
¼ cup dried currants
¼ cup tiny frozen peas, thawed
¼ cup finely diced red bell pepper
3 tablespoons chicken stock or broth
3 tablespoons finely minced red onion
2 teaspoons raspberry vinegar
2 teaspoons minced fresh mint, or ½ teaspoon dried
1 cup water

1.   Cut the zucchini in half lengthwise. Using a grapefruit spoon or a melon baller, remove the inside from the zucchini, leaving a ¼-

inch-thick shell. Discard the inside of the zucchini shells or reserve it for another use. Sprinkle the insides of the zucchini with about ½ teaspoon salt and place upside down on paper toweling. Let drain at least 30 minutes.

2.   Heat 1 tablespoon oil in the pressure cooker. Add the pine nuts and cook just until they begin to darken in color and smell fragrant, 1 to 2 minutes. Transfer to a medium bowl.

3.   Add the remaining ingredients except 1 cup water, including salt to taste, to the pine nuts and mix well. Break apart clumps of the couscous with a fork. Divide the filling among the four zucchini boats, spreading it over the entire length of the shells.

4.   Put 1 cup water in the bottom of the pressure cooker and add the trivet. Arrange the zucchini on the trivet. Cover pressure cooker and bring up to full pressure (15 pounds). Reduce heat to stabilize pressure and cook for 4 minutes. Release pressure immediately. Serve hot or at room temperature.

SHRIMP-STUFFED ARTICHOKES

Artichokes and pressure cookers were made for each other. As proof, one need only compare the cooking time required using conventional methods (50 minutes) with the time required using a pressure cooker (15 minutes). Enough said?

Instead of serving them plain, as they often are, you can fill the artichokes with a savory blend of shrimp, roasted peppers, and cheese. Serve them as a light main course for lunch or supper.

Preparation time: 20 minutes
Pressure cooking time: 15 minutes
Other cooking time: 3 minutes

Yield: 4 servings

1 lemon
4 large artichokes, about 12 ounces each
2 large cloves garlic
2 tablespoons olive oil
8 ounces tiny frozen salad shrimp, thawed
½ cup diced roasted red pepper, either fresh or from a jar

½ teaspoon coarsely cracked black pepper
Salt to taste
½ cup grated Parmesan cheese
¼ cup fresh bread crumbs
1½ cups water

1.   Remove 4 long strips (approximately 2 inches by ½ inch) of lemon zest with a vegetable peeler and set aside. Cut the lemon in half. Trim the stems of the artichokes flush with the bottoms so they stand upright. Cut off about 1½ inches from the top of each artichoke, then trim the pointed tips from all the leaves. Spread the leaves open and remove the lighter yellow leaves from the center of the artichoke. When the fuzzy choke at the center of the artichoke is exposed, use a grapefruit spoon or melon baller to scrape away the choke so only the tender artichoke bottom is left. Rub all the cut surfaces of the artichoke with lemon, including the inside.

2.   Mince the lemon zest and garlic. Heat the oil in the pressure cooker. Add the lemon zest and garlic and cook until softened, 2 to 3 minutes. Squeeze any excess water from the shrimp and add the shrimp, red pepper, black pepper, and salt to taste to the pressure cooker. Toss lightly and remove from the heat. Transfer to a bowl and add the cheese and bread crumbs.

3.   Divide the filling among the four artichokes, then wrap each one in aluminum foil so it is completely enclosed. Add 1½ cups water to the pressure cooker and put the trivet in place. Stand the wrapped artichokes on the trivet. Cover pressure cooker and bring up to full pressure (15 pounds). Reduce heat to stabilize pressure and cook for 15 minutes. Release pressure immediately. Unwrap the artichokes and serve immediately.

8
RICE, BEANS, AND PASTA

BASIC WHITE RICE

BASIC BROWN RICE

MADRAS RICE

WILD RICE AND BARLEY CASSEROLE
WITH MUSHROOMS

RICE AND WHEAT BERRY PILAF

RISOTTO WITH ASPARAGUS AND PEAS

MEXICAN RICE

BROCCOLI AND RICE AU GRATIN

ONE-STEP, ONE-POT PASTA WITH
TOMATO SAUCE

BISTRO LENTIL SALAD WITH GOAT CHEESE

NAVY BEANS WITH SAUSAGE AND HERBS

Starchy foodstuffs, from pasta to rice to dried beans, are increasingly popular at mealtime. Once erroneously scorned as being fattening "fillers," they now enjoy a status that is more in keeping with their real value. As days of high-protein meals are left behind, many dinner tables are set with less meat, more complex carbohydrates. A well-balanced diet makes room for both.

103

Over half the world favors rice as its primary grain. Interestingly, the pressure cooker is far more common in other parts of the world than it is here in the States. Savvy cooks have apparently discovered that the pressure cooker is quite an ally for quick, flawless cooking of rice.

Dried beans are now enjoying unprecedented popularity. If at one time their strong suit was that they were an inexpensive option to meat, they're playing with a stronger hand now. Inexpensive still applies, but their appeal has been bolstered by talk of low-fat meals, complex carbohydrates, and more fiber-rich diets. Dried beans boast all of these attributes, making them appealing on many different fronts. There are many varieties of dried beans, some as familiar as lima and kidney beans, others as uncommon as appaloosa and cranberry beans. All are powerhouses of protein and supply good amounts of vitamins and minerals as well. And as for soluble and insoluble fiber, beans stand out as a tremendous source of both types.

And finally, pasta is a food that shouldn't be overlooked when a quick, easy meal is called for. In addition to the pasta entrée presented in this chapter, there are several sauce recipes throughout the book that are tailor-made for piling on top of pasta.

Soaking Dried Beans

Soaking beans is optional, and some pressure cooker books make much of the fact that dried beans do not need to be soaked before cooking in the pressure cooker. This overlooks one important fact: beans are soaked not only to soften them and hasten cooking but also to remove some of their indigestible sugars—the culprits that cause flatulence.

The California Dry Bean Association has devised a method of hot soaking that increases the hydration of the beans (their ability to absorb water, crucial for cooking) and which removes 75 percent of the flatulence-causing sugars. I've become a devoted convert to their method and have adapted it to the pressure cooker.

Put 8 ounces dried beans in the pressure cooker along with 5 cups of water and 2 teaspoons salt. The salt increases the beans' ability to absorb water and cook evenly, but it can be omitted if you're on a low-sodium diet. Cover the pressure cooker and bring up to low pressure (5 pounds). When low pressure is reached, remove the cooker from the heat and release the pressure. Uncover and let stand for 4 hours. Dried beans double in volume when soaked. Drain and discard the soaking liquid. Add 4 cups fresh water. Do not add salt to the water this time. Cook as directed.

Because soaking requires planning ahead, it can play havoc with any last-minute decision to cook beans. Beans can be soaked and drained ahead of time, then wrapped tightly and held in the refrigerator for a day or two before they become sour. For longer storage, pop them into the freezer, where they can be held for several months.

Cooking Dried Beans

The range of cooking times listed on the accompanying chart are for beans that have been soaked as described above. When cooked according to these times, the beans will be tender but still have a touch of resilience and will not be at all mushy. They are suitable for salads, cooked dishes, soups, chilies, and the like. For pureeing, cook 50 percent to 100 percent longer.

After soaking the beans by the hot soak method, drain them and add 3 cups water for every 8 ounces of beans. Do not add salt. Bring up to full pressure (15 pounds), then reduce the heat and cook for the listed time. For all bean cooking, always reduce the pressure by holding the top of the pressure cooker under cold running water. If the beans are not cooked to your liking, simply replace the lock and cover and cook a bit longer.

SOAKED BEAN COOKING TIMES

Bean	Minutes after High Pressure Reached
Adzuki	5 to 7 minutes
Black turtle	7 to 9 minutes
Black-eyed peas	3 to 4 minutes
Bolita	6 to 8 minutes
Calypso	4 to 6 minutes
Chickpeas	10 to 12 minutes
Cranberry	8 to 10 minutes
Great Northern	7 to 9 minutes
Kidney	7 to 9 minutes
Brown or green lentils*	9 to 11 minutes
Red lentils*	3 to 4 minutes
Large limas	3 to 4 minutes
Small limas	3 to 5 minutes
Pigeon peas	5 to 7 minutes
Pinto	5 to 7 minutes
Navy pea	3 to 5 minutes
Rattlesnake	4 to 6 minutes
Red	4 to 6 minutes
Scarlet runner	10 to 12 minutes
Soybeans	10 to 12 minutes

*No soaking is required for lentils. Add 1 tablespoon vegetable oil to the cooking water.

BASIC WHITE RICE

Just as there is seemingly no end to the uses for plain white rice, so, too, is there seemingly no end to the ways to vary this most basic preparation. Fresh or dried herbs can be added, as can aromatic spices, some minced lemon zest along with a splash of fresh lemon juice, sautéed vegetables, and even bits of leftover meat. Chilled, the rice can be turned into a sensational salad by adding a vinaigrette dressing plus some fresh vegetables.

Preparation time: 2 minutes
Pressure cooking time: 7 minutes

Yield: 3 cups

1 cup converted long grain white rice
2 cups water or chicken stock or broth
1 tablespoon unsalted butter
½ teaspoon salt, or to taste

Combine all the ingredients in the pressure cooker and stir well. Cover pressure cooker and bring up to full pressure (15 pounds). Reduce heat to stabilize pressure and cook for 7 minutes. Release pressure under cold water, then unlock and loosen the cover. Let stand 5 minutes with the cover on but not locked. Fluff with a fork and serve immediately.

BASIC BROWN RICE

Brown rice, with the bran and hull layers still intact, contains more vitamins, minerals, and fiber than white rice. Because of these outer layers, it takes two to three times longer to cook than white rice, even in the pressure cooker. It proved to be the most variable ingredient, as far as cooking time goes, that I cooked in the pressure cooker, causing me at one point to consider avoiding mention of it altogether. Sometimes brown rice cooks much quicker than it's supposed to, while other times it stubbornly remains hard long after the prescribed cooking time. As I pondered this idiosyncrasy, I recalled that brown rice behaved much the same way when cooked in a pan. And, so it seems, variable timing is just one of those things you have to accept and work around. Check the rice after 18 minutes. It probably won't be cooked, but then again, you never know. Add more time—or more water—whatever is needed to get the job done.

If the rice is first soaked in water overnight, cooking time is drastically reduced but, alas, still unpredictable. For soaked rice, decrease the water by ½ cup and try cooking for 12 minutes. Test it and add more time if necessary. Having given my homily on brown rice, I urge you to give it a try. Besides having lots of vitamins and so on, brown rice is just plain delicious.

Preparation time: 2 minutes
Pressure cooking time: 18 to 25 minutes

Yield: 3 cups

1 cup brown rice
1¾ cups water
1 tablespoon butter or margarine
½ teaspoon salt, or to taste

Combine rice, water, butter, and salt in pressure cooker and stir well. Cover pressure cooker and bring up to full pressure (15 pounds). Reduce heat to the lowest setting that will maintain full pressure and cook for 18 minutes. Release pressure under cold water and test rice. If the rice is not tender, add additional liquid if necessary, replace cover, and cook longer—up to 25 minutes total cooking time. When rice is properly cooked, release pressure and unlock the cover. Let stand 5 minutes. Fluff with a fork and serve immediately.

MADRAS RICE

A subtle suggestion of curry and the natural sweetness of dried currants and apple are quite harmonious in this simply prepared rice dish. Serve it with grilled lamb, chicken, or duck. Or turn it into a main course by folding leftover meat into the rice.

Preparation time: 5 minutes
Pressure cooking time: 7 minutes plus 5 minutes standing time
Other cooking time: 5 minutes

Yield: 3 cups

2 medium shallots
3 tablespoons unsalted butter
1 cup long grain white rice
2 cups chicken stock or broth
¾ teaspoon curry powder
¼ teaspoon crushed red pepper flakes, or to taste
⅛ teaspoon cinnamon
Salt to taste
1 small red apple
¼ cup toasted chopped cashews
¼ cup dried currants

1.   Mince the shallots. Melt the butter in the pressure cooker and add the shallots. Cook over medium heat until they begin to soften, 3 to 4 minutes. Add the rice and cook 1 minute longer.

2.   Add the chicken stock or broth, curry powder, red pepper flakes, cinnamon, and salt to taste. Cover pressure cooker and bring up to full pressure (15 pounds). Reduce heat to stabilize pressure and cook for 7 minutes. Release pressure under cold water.

3.   While the rice is cooking, dice the unpeeled apple. When the rice has cooked, remove the cover and stir in the apple, cashews, and currants. Set the cover on the pressure cooker without locking it and let stand for 5 minutes before serving.

WILD RICE AND BARLEY CASSEROLE
WITH MUSHROOMS

Wild rice, one of the few truly native American foods, originally grew mostly in the upper midwest. Recently California and several other western states have began cultivating it with good results. Even with the increased supplies, wild rice remains costly, so here it is deliciously supplemented with bits of barley and sautéed mushrooms.

The cooking time and amount of liquid needed for wild rice vary no matter how it is cooked. After 23 minutes, you may have to replace the pressure cooker cover and add an additional minute or two of pressure cooking time. If the rice is cooked and all the liquid hasn't been absorbed, simply pour off the excess before adding the mushrooms.

Preparation time: 5 minutes
Pressure cooking time: 23 minutes
Other cooking time: 8 minutes

Yield: About 3½ cups

2 large shallots
4 tablespoons unsalted butter
¾ cup wild rice
¼ cup barley (not quick cooking)
¼ cup dry sherry
1½ cups beef stock or broth
1¼ cups water
6 ounces mushrooms, sliced
Salt to taste

1.   Mince the shallots. Melt 2 tablespoons butter in the pressure cooker. Add the shallots and cook over high heat until softened, about 2 minutes. Add the rice and barley and stir well. Pour in the sherry. When the mixture has stopped sputtering, add the beef stock or broth and water.

2.   Cover pressure cooker and bring up to full pressure (15 pounds). Reduce heat to stabilize pressure and cook for 23 minutes. Release pressure. Most of the rice should be split open and tender but not mushy. Return the cover and cook longer if necessary. If there is liquid remaining after the rice is cooked, pour it off.

3.   The mushrooms can be cooked in the pressure cooker by removing the rice after it is cooked, or they can be cooked in a skillet while the rice is cooking. Melt the remaining 2 tablespoons butter in the pressure cooker or a skillet. Add the mushrooms and cook over high heat until they are soft and most of the liquid has cooked away.

4.   Fold the mushrooms into the rice mixture and add salt to taste. This dish can be made several days in advance and refrigerated. Reheat on the stove or in the microwave oven before serving.

RICE AND WHEAT BERRY PILAF

The same grain that is ground into flour makes a wonderfully chewy and flavorful addition to rice pilaf. Wheat berries look a bit like barley but are more deeply colored. Some health food stores offer several varieties—soft or hard winter wheat, red wheat, and so on. In cooking, all are interchangeable.

Although they could simply be cooked much longer (about 25 minutes) to achieve the same results, soaking the berries overnight puts them on the same cooking schedule as white rice.

Preparation time: 2 minutes plus 12 hours soaking time
Pressure cooking time: 8 minutes

Yield: 3 cups

⅓ cup wheat berries
⅔ cup long grain white rice
2 cups water
1 tablespoon unsalted butter
½ teaspoon salt, or to taste

1.   Cover wheat berries with water and soak 12 hours. Drain well. Berries can be soaked and drained in advance and refrigerated for up to 2 days or frozen.

2.   Combine wheat berries, rice, water, butter, and salt to taste in pressure cooker and stir well. Cover pressure cooker and bring up to full pressure (15 pounds). Reduce heat to stabilize pressure and cook for 8 minutes. Release pressure by holding pan under cold water. Open cover but do not remove, and let stand 5 minutes. Fluff with fork and serve immediately.

RISOTTO WITH ASPARAGUS AND PEAS

Risotto, a classic Milanese rice preparation, typically requires about 30 minutes of constant stirring and fussing to achieve its characteristic creamy texture. In the pressure cooker, the same wonderful results are obtained with a minimum of bother and in much less time. Arborio rice is necessary for authentic risotto. If you can't find it, the recipe can be prepared with converted long grain rice, although it won't be quite the same.

Preparation time: 10 minutes
Pressure cooking time: 8 minutes
Other cooking time: 5 minutes

Yield: 3 cups

1 small onion, 2 ounces
2 tablespoons unsalted butter
1 cup arborio rice
⅓ cup dry white wine
2 cups chicken stock or broth
6 to 7 slender asparagus spears
½ cup tiny peas
¼ cup grated Parmesan cheese
2 tablespoons minced fresh parsley, preferably flat leaf
Salt and freshly ground black pepper to taste

1.   Dice the onion. Melt the butter in pressure cooker and add the onion. Cook over medium heat until the onion becomes translucent, about 2 minutes. Add the rice, stir well, and cook 2 minutes. Slowly pour in wine and cook until it has evaporated.

2.   Add chicken stock or broth. Cover pressure cooker and bring up to full pressure (15 pounds). Reduce heat to stabilize pressure and cook for 8 minutes. Remove from stove and let pressure come down on its own accord.

3.   Meanwhile, trim ends from asparagus and peel spears with a vegetable peeler. Cut on the bias into ½-inch-thick slices.

4.   Uncover pressure cooker and add asparagus, peas, Parmesan cheese, and parsley. Add salt and pepper to taste and serve hot.

MEXICAN RICE

Here's an easy way to make a sassy side dish that enhances any Mexican or Tex-Mex meal. Use a mild salsa rather than one that is hot unless you want the rice to be a scorcher.

Preparation time: 5 minutes
Pressure cooking time: 7 minutes

Yield: 3 cups

1 small onion, about 3 ounces
2 slices bacon
1 cup long grain white rice
1¾ cups chicken stock or broth
¾ cup bottled salsa
¼ cup tiny frozen peas, thawed
¼ cup minced fresh cilantro
Salt to taste

1.   Dice the onion and cut the bacon into small pieces. The bacon will be easier to cut if it is semifrozen.

2.   Cook the bacon and onion in the pressure cooker until the bacon is browned. Stir in the rice and cook 1 minute. Add the stock or broth and salsa. Cover pressure cooker and bring up to full pressure (15 pounds). Reduce heat to stabilize pressure and cook for 7 minutes. Release the pressure and add the peas, cilantro, and salt to taste. Serve hot.

BROCCOLI AND RICE AU GRATIN

Creamy, rich, and generously flecked with fresh broccoli, this is a marvelous side dish for simple grilled or broiled meats. The cheese will thicken as it stands. Thin it with additional milk if it becomes too thick. Finely diced water chestnuts or diced and drained tomatoes can be stirred in along with the cheese if desired.

Preparation time: 10 minutes
Pressure cooking time: 6 minutes
Other cooking time: 5 minutes

Yield: About 3½ cups

1 small onion, about 2 ounces
2 tablespoons unsalted butter
1 cup long grain white rice
1¼ cups chicken stock or broth
1 cup milk
Dash red pepper sauce
1 large stalk broccoli
1 cup (4 ounces) shredded Monterey Jack cheese
¼ cup minced parsley
Freshly grated nutmeg to taste
Salt and freshly ground black pepper to taste

1.   Mince the onion. Melt the butter in the pressure cooker. Add the onion and cook until it is soft, about 4 minutes. Add the rice and cook 1 minute longer. Add the stock or broth, milk, and red pepper sauce. Cover pressure cooker and bring up to full pressure (15 pounds). Reduce heat to stabilize pressure and cook for 5 minutes.

2.   While the rice is cooking, finely mince the broccoli. After the rice has cooked for 5 minutes, release pressure by holding the cooker under cold water. Add the broccoli and replace the cover. Bring back to full pressure (15 pounds) and cook 1 minute longer.

3.   Release the pressure and stir in the cheese, parsley, nutmeg, and salt and pepper to taste. Serve immediately.

ONE-STEP, ONE-POT PASTA WITH TOMATO SAUCE

No, there's no mistake here. The pasta isn't cooked first. Instead, it goes into the sauce—still raw—and cooks at the same time the sauce simmers, emerging from the pot perfectly al dente and full of flavor. It ends up like baked pasta—thick, rich, and tomatoey. Instead of grated cheese, diced mozzarella or fontina can be folded into the pasta after it is cooked.

Preparation time: 10 minutes
Pressure cooking time: 12 minutes
Other cooking time: 4 minutes

Yield: 2 main course or 4 side dish servings

1 large clove garlic
1 medium onion, about 5 ounces
3 tablespoons olive oil
8 ounces rigatoni or mostaccioli pasta
2 cups prepared spaghetti sauce or Bolognese sauce
1½ cups beef stock or broth
1 tablespoon balsamic or red wine vinegar
Crushed red pepper flakes
Salt and freshly ground black pepper to taste
½ teaspoon dried basil, or 2 tablespoons fresh
½ teaspoon dried oregano, or 2 tablespoons fresh
Grated Parmesan or Romano cheese, about ¼ cup

1.   Mince the garlic and chop the onion. Heat the oil in the pressure cooker. When it is hot, add the garlic and onion and cook until softened, 3 to 4 minutes. Stir in the pasta, spaghetti sauce, stock or broth, vinegar, red pepper flakes, and salt and pepper to taste. If you are using dried basil and oregano, add them now as well.

2.   Cover pressure cooker and bring up to full pressure (15 pounds). Reduce heat to stabilize pressure and cook for 12 minutes. Release pressure. Add fresh basil and oregano, if used, and serve with grated cheese.

BISTRO LENTIL SALAD WITH GOAT CHEESE

This salad is light enough for summertime meals, yet sturdy enough to anchor a winter repast. French-style goat cheese lends its characteristic tang, which goes well with the peppery taste of lentils. A confetti of diced vegetables adds crunch and fresh flavors.

Be sure to use brown or green lentils. Red and yellow lentils quickly become too mushy to use in a salad. Lentils have a tendency to foam during cooking in the pressure cooker. Tossing them with oil before cooking helps to minimize the foaming.

Preparation time: 10 minutes
Pressure cooking time: 10 minutes

Yield: 3 to 4 servings

1 cup brown or green lentils
6 tablespoons olive oil
2 cups water
1½ tablespoons sherry wine vinegar
1 tablespoon Dijon mustard
¼ teaspoon ground cumin
¼ teaspoon sugar
Salt and freshly ground black pepper to taste
1 medium red onion, 3 to 4 ounces
½ small red bell pepper
½ small orange or green bell pepper
1 small jalapeño or serrano pepper
¼ cup fresh cilantro or fresh mint leaves
4 ounces soft goat cheese

1.   Put lentils in pressure cooker and add 1 tablespoon oil. Stir so they are well coated, then add the water. Cover pressure cooker and bring up to full pressure (15 pounds). Reduce heat to stabilize pressure and cook for 10 minutes. Release pressure by holding the cooker under cold running water. Remove the cover, transfer the lentils to a colander, and drain thoroughly. Place in a large bowl.

2.   Put vinegar, mustard, cumin, sugar, and salt and pepper to taste in a small dish and stir until the salt dissolves. Add the remaining 5 tablespoons olive oil and mix well. Add the dressing to

the warm lentils and let stand until they have cooled to room temperature.

3.   Meanwhile, dice the onion. Dice the bell peppers to about the size of the lentils. Remove all seeds and ribs from the jalapeño and mince. Mince the cilantro.

4.   When the lentils are cool, add the vegetables, jalapeño, and cilantro and mix gently. Crumble the cheese into the salad and mix lightly so the cheese stays in pieces. Serve immediately or refrigerate overnight. Adjust the seasoning before serving.

NAVY BEANS WITH SAUSAGE AND HERBS

Beans have a rustic character that makes them fit companions to boldly flavored foods such as sausage. This collaboration proves the point. Barely cooked vegetables and fresh herbs add texture and colorful accents to the tiny white beans and slices of sausage. This dish can be served hot or can be chilled, then served at room temperature. If you serve it at room temperature, play up the salad side of it by serving it on lettuce leaves and adding a garnish of fresh herbs.

Preparation time: 15 minutes
Pressure cooking time: 4 minutes
Other cooking time: 15 minutes

Yield: 4 cups

8 ounces dried navy beans
3 cups water
12 ounces Italian link sausages (about 3)
3 tablespoons olive oil
½ small fennel bulb, or 1 medium stalk celery
1 small red onion, about 3 ounces
1 small red bell pepper, about 4 ounces
1 teaspoon dried sage
1 tablespoon fresh lemon juice, or more to taste
3 tablespoons minced fresh herbs (preferably basil or oregano, but
  parsley if others aren't in season)
Salt and coarsely cracked black pepper to taste

1.   Soak the beans as directed (see Index). Drain and place in the pressure cooker with 3 cups water. Cover pressure cooker and bring up to full pressure (15 pounds). Reduce heat to stabilize pressure and cook for 4 minutes, or slightly longer if you prefer softer beans. Release pressure immediately and drain the beans thoroughly.

2.   In the pressure cooker, cook the sausage in water to cover over medium-high heat until it is no longer pink in the center, about 10 minutes. Spill off the water, add 1 tablespoon oil, and brown the sausage on all sides. Set aside.

3.   Dice the fennel or celery, onion, and bell pepper. Heat the remaining 2 tablespoons oil. Add the vegetables and sage and cook over high heat for 2 minutes. Transfer to a mixing bowl and add the beans, lemon juice, and herbs. Slice the sausage and add to mixture, along with salt and pepper to taste. Serve warm or at room temperature.

9
SAUCES

■

DEEP, RICH, RED BARBECUE SAUCE

BOLOGNESE SAUCE

ROASTED RED PEPPER AND TOMATO SAUCE

CHILE VERDE SAUCE

SPICY FRUIT BARBECUE SAUCE

Sauces are one of the cook's special "tools." They turn the mundane into the remarkable, the everyday into the special. Consider that eggs Benedict is just ham and eggs without the luxurious addition of hollandaise sauce, steak Bordelaise is just grilled beef until the wine-enriched sauce is napped over the top, and spaghetti is just plain spaghetti until that gorgeous red meat sauce is ladled over it.

Although some sauce recipes develop their fullest and best flavor only through long simmering in an open kettle, there are many sauce recipes that are ideal for cooking in the pressure cooker. A highly versatile selection of these follows, with each promising to make meals easy, varied, and always interesting. All can be made at least 5 days ahead of time and used as the need arises to add a special touch to a last-minute meal.

DEEP, RICH, RED BARBECUE SAUCE

This is the kind of barbecue sauce to slather over ribs and chicken and then lick up every last bit from lips and fingers. Thick, sweet, tangy, smoky, and ever so slightly spicy, it can be mixed with cooked pork for the most heavenly barbecue sandwiches, stirred into mayonnaise for a sandwich spread, or added to sour cream for a quick chip dip.

Preparation time: 10 minutes
Pressure cooking time: 20 minutes

Yield: 2 cups

1 small onion, about 3 ounces
1 cup tomato sauce
⅔ cup catsup
½ cup cider vinegar
½ cup light brown sugar
4 tablespoons unsalted butter
2 tablespoons molasses
2 tablespoons corn syrup
1 tablespoon liquid smoke
1 tablespoon Dijon mustard
6 to 8 dashes red pepper sauce
1 tablespoon dark rum, if desired

1.   Mince the onion. Transfer to pressure cooker and add tomato sauce, catsup, vinegar, brown sugar, butter, molasses, corn syrup, liquid smoke, mustard, and red pepper sauce.

2.   Cover pressure cooker and bring up to full pressure (15 pounds). Reduce heat to stabilize pressure and cook for 20 minutes. Release pressure and add rum, if desired. Sauce can be refrigerated for up to a week or frozen.

BOLOGNESE SAUCE

This is a classic Italian meat sauce, prepared with a number of modifications that acknowledge modern tastes and cooking trends. Traditionally, it is made with a large piece of meat that is removed after cooking and either shredded and added to the sauce or served with another meal. Here, ground meat, including some spicy sausage, is used instead. Hours of stove-top simmering are replaced by 15 quick minutes in the pressure cooker along with a small amount of additional time on the stove. The result is a robust, hearty sauce that is superb over pasta or as a sauce in countless Italian preparations.

The cream may seem to be an odd ingredient. It was suggested with a knowing wink by a very able Italian cook as a way to add a smooth, round finish to the sauce, and it does just that. It can certainly be omitted if you prefer.

Preparation time: 15 minutes
Pressure cooking time: 15 minutes
Other cooking time: 15 minutes

Yield: 8 cups

1 pound lean ground beef
½ pound bulk hot or mild Italian sausage
2 large cloves garlic
2 medium onions, about 10 ounces total
1 large carrot
1 large stalk celery
1 28-ounce can chopped tomatoes in puree
1 6-ounce can tomato paste
½ cup dry red wine
2 teaspoons dried basil
¾ teaspoon dried oregano
¾ teaspoon sugar
8 ounces small mushrooms, trimmed and quartered
Salt and freshly ground black pepper to taste
¾ cup cream or half-and-half, if desired

1.   Crumble the beef and sausage in the pressure cooker and cook until well browned. Spill off all but a small amount of the fat and leave the meat in the pan.

2.   While the meat is browning, prepare the vegetables. If you have a food processor, mince the garlic in it, then chop the onions, carrot, and celery, or chop the vegetables by hand.

3.   When the meat is browned, stir in the vegetables and cook 2 minutes. Add the tomatoes, tomato paste, wine, basil, oregano, and sugar. Cover pressure cooker and bring up to full pressure (15 pounds). Reduce heat to stabilize pressure and cook for 15 minutes.

4.   Release pressure and add the mushrooms and salt and pepper to taste. Cook, uncovered, until mushrooms are just tender, about 5 minutes. Add cream, if desired, and adjust seasoning. The sauce can be refrigerated for up to 4 days or frozen.

ROASTED RED PEPPER AND TOMATO SAUCE

In mid- to late July, the price of red peppers falls drastically and a bumper crop of tomatoes finds its way to the market. This sauce celebrates the seasonal abundance of both of these rosy red treats. Though it is a bit more time-consuming to prepare than many recipes in this book, it is a worthwhile effort. The intensely flavored sauce can be used to top off grilled meat or fish, added to steamed vegetables, or used as a low-calorie topping for pasta. Depending on how indulgent you're feeling, a tablespoon or two of butter can be whisked in at serving time for a rich finish. The recipe can easily be doubled, which is especially helpful since the sauce freezes very well.

Preparation time: 20 minutes
Pressure cooking time: 20 minutes
Other cooking time: 20 minutes

Yield: 2½ cups

1½ pounds red bell peppers
2¼ pounds vine-ripened plum tomatoes
1 to 2 large cloves garlic
1 tablespoon olive oil
2 tablespoons tomato paste

¹/₂ teaspoon sugar, or more, depending on the tomatoes
Crushed red pepper flakes to taste
Salt to taste

1.   Roast the red peppers by placing them over an open flame and turning them as necessary until the skin is completely blackened. Or, cut the peppers lengthwise, trimming them so they lie flat. Arrange, cut side down, on a foil-lined baking sheet and broil close to the heat until blackened. After roasting, transfer the peppers to a paper bag, seal tightly, and let stand until the peppers are cool enough to handle. Peel off the skin, rinsing the peppers under cold water to remove any bits of blackened skin. Core and seed the peppers and chop rough.

2.   Peel the tomatoes by dropping them into a large pot of boiling water and cook them about 30 seconds—just until the skins loosen. Core them and slip off the skins. Cut in half crosswise and squeeze gently to remove the seeds. Chop rough.

3.   Mince the garlic. Heat the oil in the pressure cooker. Add the garlic and cook until it is soft, 2 to 3 minutes. Add the tomatoes, bell peppers, tomato paste, sugar, and red pepper flakes. Cover pressure cooker and bring up to full pressure (15 pounds). Reduce heat to stabilize pressure and cook for 20 minutes. Release the pressure and remove the cover. Boil vigorously until the sauce is thick, 15 to 20 minutes, stirring often toward the end so it does not stick. Add salt to taste, as well as more sugar if necessary. The sauce can be refrigerated for up to 4 days or frozen.

CHILE VERDE SAUCE

Not for the timid, this sauce is for those who like to take a walk on the wild side. It's hot and sassy, full of south-of-the-border zing. More like a cooked salsa than a smooth sauce, it has any number of uses—as a salsa, with eggs, over enchiladas, in stews. It's a great addition to any meal that needs a little spicing up.

Peppers vary widely in how hot they are. At times, poblanos will be quite docile, while other times will find them most intemperate. To avoid ending up with a sauce that's too tame, roast a serrano pepper and add as much as necessary to make a sauce that's hot but not a scorcher.

Preparation time: 20 minutes
Pressure cooking time: 10 minutes
Other cooking time: 5 minutes

Yield: 1½ cups

6 large poblano peppers
2 large green bell peppers
1 serrano or jalapeño pepper, if desired
1 medium onion, about 4 ounces
1 large clove garlic
2 tablespoons vegetable oil
⅓ cup chicken stock or broth
1 teaspoon cumin seeds
½ teaspoon sugar
Salt to taste
½ cup fresh minced cilantro

1.   Roast all the peppers by placing them over an open flame until they are completely blackened on all sides. Transfer the roasted peppers to a paper bag, seal tightly, and let stand until the peppers are cool enough to handle. Peel the skins off, running the peppers under cold water if necessary to remove all the blackened bits. Remove the core and seeds and dice the poblano and bell peppers and mince the serrano.

2.   Mince the onion and garlic. Heat the oil in the pressure cooker over high heat. Add the garlic and onions and cook, stirring often, until soft, about 5 minutes.

3.   Add the diced peppers, stock or broth, cumin seeds, sugar, and salt to taste. Cover pressure cooker and bring up to full

pressure (15 pounds). Reduce heat to stabilize pressure and cook for 10 minutes. Release pressure and add the cilantro. The sauce can be refrigerated for up to 4 days.

SPICY FRUIT BARBECUE SAUCE

This sauce has a pleasingly complex mix of flavor sensations—hot peppers playing off sweet summer fruits and a bit of salty soy sauce tamed by honey and warm spices. It can be used on chicken, duck, pork, shrimp, and even lamb.

Preparation time: 10 minutes
Pressure cooking time: 15 minutes

Yield: 2 cups

1 large clove garlic
1 small jalapeño or serrano pepper
1 piece ginger, about 3/4-inch cube
1 small onion, about 2 ounces, quartered
1 16-ounce can tart cherries
1 16-ounce can pitted plums
1/4 cup honey
3 tablespoons seasoned rice vinegar
1 tablespoon dark soy sauce
2 whole allspice berries
1 cinnamon stick

1.   Mince the garlic, jalapeño, ginger, and onion in a food processor. Drain the cherries and plums and add the fruit to the processor along with honey, vinegar, and soy sauce. Process with on and off turns until the ingredients are just mixed and the fruit is chopped coarsely. Do not puree the fruit.

2.   Transfer mixture to the pressure cooker and add allspice and cinnamon. Cover pressure cooker and bring up to full pressure (15 pounds). Reduce heat to stabilize pressure and cook for 15 minutes. Release pressure. Sauce can be refrigerated for up to 5 days or frozen. Remove allspice and cinnamon before serving.

Note: Seasoned rice vinegar, also called sushi vinegar, is rice vinegar that has been seasoned with sugar and salt. It is available in some large supermarkets, specialty food stores, and Oriental markets.

10
DESSERTS

■

BANANA CUSTARDS

NEVER-FAIL FLAN

CREME DE LA CREME CHEESECAKE

CREAMY MOCHA CHEESECAKE

APPLE-CURRANT STEAMED PUDDING

DOUBLE-DARK CHOCOLATE STEAMED PUDDING

STEWED WINTER FRUIT COMPOTE

NEW ENGLAND BROWN BREAD

PUMPKIN BREAD PUDDING

OLD-FASHIONED BREAD PUDDING
WITH CARAMEL SAUCE

The thought of a cookbook without a chapter on desserts seems downright un-American to me. Fortunately, even though desserts and pressure cookers seem to be a most unlikely match, the pressure cooker does have its sweet side. While cookies, pies, and cakes will always be left to the oven, there are several all-time dessert favorites that the pressure cooker does especially well. Exquisite cheesecakes, extra-rich bread puddings, silky-smooth custards, moist steamed puddings, and perfectly poached fruits are all within the realm of pressure cookers. And, true to form, they cook more quickly in the pressure cooker than they do by conventional methods.

Depending on how often you use your pressure cooker for making desserts, you may find it worthwhile to invest in several baking dishes that fit inside the pressure cooker. A 7-inch springform pan fits neatly inside most 6-quart cookers. If you already have an 8-inch springform pan in your collection, see if it fits in your pressure cooker. Some fit very easily, while others just don't make it. If you use an 8-inch springform, cooking times will likely be less than indicated in the recipes that follow. Adjust the timing accordingly. A 6-cup soufflé dish is also enormously versatile. In addition, I use a round, 6-cup pudding mold that is deeper than a baking dish and somewhat smaller in circumference. A ring mold is nice to have as well, if only to make the most luscious flan in the world. Individual soufflé dishes or custard cups are useful, too. Any of these pieces should be easy to come by in a well-stocked kitchenware department.

No matter how you cook desserts, timing is critical. Custards are especially delicate and require close attention and gentle cooking. This chapter includes some unusual instructions that aren't found elsewhere in the book. Any recipe that calls for leavening agents is started *without* pressure. The superheated high-pressure atmosphere is too much for baking soda or baking powder. Thus, these desserts are started over very low pressure or without any at all. Then, after the leavening has had plenty of time to act, the cover is locked into place for a faster finish.

BANANA CUSTARDS

These silky-smooth custards take on a tropical taste with the addition of pureed banana and dark rum. Served warm, they're sensational with a light chocolate sauce. If you're serving them cold, try a raspberry puree, or go exotic and sauce them with sweetened passion fruit or pureed papaya.

Be sure not to overcook the custards. Carefully maintain the pressure at 5 pounds so the texture stays smooth.

Preparation time: 15 minutes
Pressure cooking time: 12 minutes

Yield: 4 servings

1 medium, very ripe banana
2 large egg yolks
1 large egg
3 tablespoons sugar
½ cup half-and-half
¼ cup sweetened condensed milk
¼ cup sour cream
1½ teaspoons dark rum
½ teaspoon pure vanilla extract
2 cups water

1.   Have four 6-ounce soufflé dishes on hand. Puree the banana in a food processor or blender. Add the egg yolks, egg, and sugar and mix until smooth. Add half-and-half, condensed milk, sour cream, rum, and vanilla and mix well. Strain mixture through a fine strainer. Transfer to soufflé dishes and cover tightly with aluminum foil.

2.   Add 2 cups of water to bottom of pressure cooker. Insert steamer basket and add soufflé dishes. The water should not reach the steamer. Add the trivet if necessary to keep the water from touching the dishes. Cover pressure cooker and bring up to low pressure (5 pounds). Reduce heat to a very low setting to stabilize pressure and cook for 12 minutes. Release pressure immediately and remove soufflé dishes. Uncover immediately. To store in the refrigerator, cool them, uncovered, to lukewarm. Cover and refrigerate for up to 2 days.

NEVER-FAIL FLAN

Flan is a rich, firm custard capped off by a light caramel sauce that cooks along with the custard. It is often served at Mexican or Spanish meals, but almost any meal that calls for dessert ends on a happy note when flan is brought to the table. Traditionally, flan is served plain, but a handful of fresh berries is a lovely complement.

Preparation time: 5 minutes
Pressure cooking time: 20 minutes
Other cooking time: 5 minutes

Yield: 8 servings

½ cup plus ⅓ cup sugar
⅛ teaspoon ground clove
2 large eggs
5 large egg yolks
1 14-ounce can sweetened condensed milk
1 12-ounce can evaporated milk
1 cup whole milk
2 teaspoons pure vanilla extract
2 cups water

1.   Have on hand a 6½-cup ring mold that will fit easily inside a pressure cooker. Cook ½ cup sugar and the clove over medium-low heat in a small heavy skillet until completely melted and a rich golden color. Immediately pour into ring mold. Holding the mold with a pot holder, tip it so the caramel spreads out into a thin layer over the entire bottom surface. Set aside.

2.   Whisk the eggs, egg yolks, and remaining ⅓ cup sugar until smooth and light. Add the remaining ingredients except for the water and mix well. Pour into ring mold. Cover tightly with aluminum foil so no water can get inside. Put 2 cups water in bottom of pressure cooker. Place the ring mold inside the steamer basket and add to pressure cooker. Cover pressure cooker and bring up to full pressure (15 pounds). Reduce heat to stabilize pressure and cook for 20 minutes. Release pressure and remove the foil. Let cool to room temperature. Flan is usually served chilled, but it can be served as soon as it comes to room temperature, if desired. It can also be refrigerated for up to 3 days. To serve, loosen from the sides of the mold with a knife and invert flan onto a serving plate. Spoon remaining caramel sauce from the bottom of the pan over the flan.

CREME DE LA CREME CHEESECAKE

Cheesecakes are immune to the fads and fashions of cooking and easily stay right at the top of a long list of dessert favorites. A creamy, smooth texture and rich taste are their big draws, and judged by those standards, this cheesecake is a big winner. The sour cream topping can be replaced by or joined with fresh seasonal berries.

Preparation time: 10 minutes, plus 12 hours refrigeration time
Pressure cooking time: 40 minutes
Yield: One 7-inch cake, 6 to 8 servings

24 ounces cream cheese (3 8-ounce packages)
1¼ cups sugar
4 large eggs
½ cup whipping cream
2 tablespoons flour
2 teaspoons pure vanilla extract
Unsalted butter, about 1 tablespoon
2 cups water

Topping (*if desired*)

1 cup sour cream
2 tablespoons sugar
1 teaspoon pure vanilla extract

1.   Combine the cream cheese and sugar in a food processor. Mix until completely smooth, scraping down the sides of the bowl several times. Add the eggs and process 1 minute longer. Add the cream, flour, and vanilla and mix thoroughly.

2.   Transfer to a buttered 7-inch springform pan. Wrap entire pan in aluminum foil so no water can get inside. Put 2 cups water in bottom of pressure cooker and add the trivet. Place cheesecake on trivet. Cover pressure cooker and bring up to full pressure (15 pounds). Reduce heat to stabilize pressure and cook for 40 minutes. Release pressure and carefully remove pan. Uncover and cool to room temperature. Cover and refrigerate overnight before serving.

3.   To make topping, if desired, stir sour cream, sugar, and vanilla together. Spread over top of chilled cheesecake.

CREAMY MOCHA CHEESECAKE

As if the mere mention of cheesecake isn't tempting enough! When chocolate is added to the concoction, all resolve crumbles and even the most stringent dieter is likely to give in to the rapture.

Preparation time: 10 minutes, plus 6 hours refrigeration time
Pressure cooking time: 40 minutes
Yield: One 7-inch cake, 6 to 8 servings

3 ounces semisweet chocolate
1 pound (two 8-ounce packages) cream cheese
1 cup packed light brown sugar
4 large eggs
1 cup sour cream
3 tablespoons double-strength coffee, cooled
2 tablespoons flour
1 teaspoon pure vanilla extract
2 cups water
Chocolate shot (jimmies), if desired

1.   Melt the chocolate in the top of a double boiler or in a microwave oven. Set aside to cool.

2.   Mix the cream cheese and brown sugar in a food processor until completely smooth. Add the eggs and mix 2 minutes, stopping several times to scrape down the sides of the bowl with a rubber spatula. Add the sour cream, coffee, flour, vanilla, and melted chocolate and mix 1 minute longer or until mixture is completely smooth.

3.   Transfer to a 7-inch springform pan. Wrap completely in aluminum foil so no water can get inside. Put 2 cups water in the bottom of the pressure cooker. Add the springform, placed in the steamer basket. Cover pressure cooker and bring up to full pressure (15 pounds). Reduce heat to stabilize pressure and cook for 40 minutes. Release pressure. When properly cooked, the cake should be set at the edges, though still slightly soft in the center. Cool to room temperature, then refrigerate at least 6 hours before serving. Remove from the pan and press chocolate shot onto the sides of the cake if desired.

Note: To make double-strength coffee, use twice the normal ratio of coffee to water.

APPLE-CURRANT STEAMED PUDDING

Steamed puddings are not at all what we typically think of as a pudding, but rather they're very much like a dense, moist cake generously laden with bits of fresh and dried fruit. They're wonderfully homey and make a sensational dessert served warm with whipped cream or a custard sauce. Cooking them in the pressure cooker is a two-step process. First, they are steamed without any pressure. Then, after they've risen, the pressure's on and they'll cook in about half the usual time.

Preparation time: 20 minutes, plus 12 hours marinating time
Pressure cooking time: 30 minutes
Other cooking time: 25 minutes

Yield: 6 servings

½ cup dried currants
2 tablespoons bourbon or brandy, or water
1½ pounds tart cooking apples
1 stick (8 tablespoons) unsalted butter, softened
½ cup plus 2 tablespoons packed light brown sugar
⅛ teaspoon ground clove
Freshly grated nutmeg to taste
2 teaspoons pure vanilla extract
3 large eggs
⅓ cup unbleached all-purpose flour
¾ teaspoon baking soda
¼ teaspoon salt
1 cup finely crushed vanilla cookie crumbs
4 cups water

1.   Combine the currants and bourbon or water in a small plastic food bag and let stand overnight or longer, or soften in a microwave oven for 35 to 40 seconds.

2.   Peel and core the apples and dice into ⅜-inch cubes. Melt 4 tablespoons butter in the pressure cooker. Add the apples and cook over high heat for 5 minutes. Add ¼ cup of the brown sugar, clove, and nutmeg to taste and cook until most of the liquid has cooked away, about 5 minutes longer. Remove from heat and add the vanilla. Set aside.

3.   In a large bowl, beat the remaining 4 tablespoons butter and remaining ¼ cup plus 2 tablespoons brown sugar until smooth. Add

the eggs one at a time, beating well after each addition. Add the flour, baking soda, and salt and mix well, then fold in the cookie crumbs, currants, and apples.

4.   Transfer to a buttered 6-cup mold. Cover with buttered aluminum foil, then wrap in foil so water can't get into pudding. Put 4 cups water in bottom of pressure cooker. Place pudding mold in the steamer basket and add to pressure cooker. Cover the pressure cooker but do not seal it. Bring to a boil, then simmer 25 minutes. Remove the cover to check the water level, adding more as necessary. Cover and lock pressure cooker and bring up to full pressure (15 pounds). Reduce heat to stabilize pressure and cook 30 minutes longer.

5.   Release pressure, remove the mold from the pressure cooker, and cool for 10 minutes. Uncover and invert onto a serving plate. Serve warm with whipped cream or custard sauce. The pudding can be made several days in advance and reheated. To do so, cook as above and cool completely in mold, then refrigerate. Return to steamer basket in pressure cooker and add 3 cups water. Bring to full pressure (15 pounds), then cook for 10 minutes.

DOUBLE-DARK CHOCOLATE STEAMED PUDDING

Goodly amounts of chocolate, dates, coconut, and macadamia nuts add up to a dense, rich delight.

Preparation time: 15 minutes
Pressure cooking time: 30 minutes
Other cooking time: 20 minutes

Yield: 6 servings

3½ ounces unsweetened chocolate
4 cups water
1 teaspoon baking soda
½ teaspoon salt
½ cup granulated sugar
½ cup packed light brown sugar
5 tablespoons unsalted butter, softened
1 large egg

1 tablespoon dark rum, or 1 teaspoon pure vanilla extract
1¾ cups unbleached all-purpose flour
½ cup chopped macadamia nuts
½ cup chopped dates
½ cup flaked coconut
Sweetened whipped cream or ice cream, if desired

1.   Melt the chocolate with 1 cup water on the stove or in the microwave oven. Stir in the baking soda and salt and set aside to cool.

2.   Cream the sugars with the butter until smooth. Beat in the egg, then the rum or vanilla. Alternately mix in the chocolate mixture and the flour, mixing until smooth. Fold in the nuts, dates, and coconut.

3.   Transfer to a buttered 6-cup pudding mold or baking dish. Cover completely with aluminum foil so no water can get inside. Put remaining 3 cups water in the bottom of the pressure cooker and put the trivet in place. Place the mold on the trivet. Put the cover in place but do not lock it. Cook, without pressure, for 20 minutes. Check the water level and add enough so the water comes up to the bottom of the trivet. Lock the cover in place and bring to full pressure (15 pounds). Reduce heat to stabilize pressure and cook for 30 minutes. Remove the pressure cooker from the heat and let it stand until the pressure drops of its own accord. Carefully remove the foil, making sure no water gets into the pudding. Serve warm or at room temperature with sweetened whipped cream or ice cream, if desired.

STEWED WINTER FRUIT COMPOTE

Warm, sweet spices and sunny citrus flavors prove to be very flattering to dried fruits. Cooked, the fruits become pleasingly plump and full of tang. The compote is delightful plain, but a selection of fresh fruit can be added after the dried fruits are cooked. The hot syrup will soften them just enough.

Packages of mixed dried fruit, which usually include apricots, prunes, apples, and pears, are the most convenient to use, providing, of course, that the selection suits your taste. A handful of dried cherries and blueberries or some dried peaches add a seductive hint of summer.

Preparation time: 10 minutes plus 10 minutes standing time
Pressure cooking time: 3 minutes

Yield: 4 servings

1 large lemon
1 large orange
1 cup water
¼ cup sugar
1 tablespoon honey
1 slice fresh ginger, about the size of a quarter and twice as thick
1 cinnamon stick
¼ teaspoon whole coriander seeds
2½ cups mixed dried fruit
1 tablespoon orange liqueur, if desired
1 cup fresh fruit, such as diced apples or pears, seedless grapes
  or pineapple, if desired

1.   Remove with a vegetable peeler 3 long strips (approximately 2½ inches by ½ inch each) of zest from both the lemon and the orange, then squeeze the juice from the fruit. Combine the zest, juice, water, sugar, honey, ginger, cinnamon stick, and coriander seeds in the pressure cooker and stir to dissolve the sugar. Add the dried fruit.

2.   Cover pressure cooker and bring up to full pressure (15 pounds). Reduce heat to stabilize pressure and cook for 3 minutes. Release pressure and add the liqueur and fresh fruit, if used. Let stand at least 10 minutes before serving, or cover tightly and refrigerate for up to 2 days if fresh fruit has been added or up to 10

days if the mixture contains only dried fruit. Remove the cinnamon and ginger just before serving.

NEW ENGLAND BROWN BREAD

Brown bread typically has the appellation of Boston preceding its name, indicating not only origin but style as well. This version replaces molasses with the lighter taste of maple and adds a bit of cornmeal for an interesting textural variation. Little bits of dried cherries and dates are a delightful addition.

The two-step cooking is important. The initial low-pressure cooking allows the leavening to do its job, so a higher pressure can be implemented to speed up cooking. Serve the bread with sweet butter or whipped cream cheese.

Preparation time: 15 minutes
Pressure cooking time: 50 minutes

Yield: 1 loaf

Unsalted butter, about 2 tablespoons
1½ cups unbleached all-purpose flour
1 cup whole wheat flour
½ cup yellow cornmeal
1½ teaspoons baking soda
¾ teaspoon baking powder
½ teaspoon salt
2 large eggs
¼ cup packed light brown sugar
4 tablespoons unsalted butter, melted
1 cup buttermilk
½ cup maple syrup
½ cup chopped dates
½ cup dried cherries
3 cups water

1.   Butter a 6-cup pudding mold or baking dish. Butter aluminum foil to fit over the container.

2.   Place both flours, cornmeal, baking soda, baking powder, and salt in a bowl and stir to combine. Set aside.

3.   Crack the eggs into a mixing bowl and beat lightly. Add

brown sugar and mix well. Stir in melted butter, buttermilk, and maple syrup. Add dry ingredients and fruits and mix until combined.

4.   Transfer to prepared dish. Cover with foil, fitting it loosely over the top so the bread has room to rise. Tie securely around edge of dish with kitchen twine.

5.   Put 3 cups of water in bottom of pressure cooker. Place pan on trivet or in steamer basket. Cover pressure cooker and bring up to the lowest pressure (5 pounds). Reduce heat to a very low setting to stabilize pressure and cook for 30 minutes. This low setting will allow the bread to rise. After 30 minutes, increase heat and allow pressure to build to 10 pounds. Stabilize at 10 pounds and cook 20 minutes longer. Release pressure and carefully remove pan from steamer. Remove foil and test with a wooden pick. If pick comes out wet, cover pan with foil, return it to pressure cooker, and cook 5 minutes longer at 10 pounds pressure. Cool in pan 10 minutes, then loosen from sides of pan with a small knife and invert onto a cooling rack. The bread is best served warm, though it can be wrapped tightly and held overnight.

PUMPKIN BREAD PUDDING

Comfort foods have become an elixir for legions of fans who welcome the chance to make a brief visit to childhood via their favorite foods. Here, the warm, fall flavors of pumpkin, cinnamon, and brandy enhance a rich, sweet, comforting custard. The pudding can be served plain or topped with a big dollop of lightly sweetened whipped cream flavored with brandy.

For best results, the bread used in this recipe should be fairly well dried out, though not hard. If it is too fresh, put it in a 200°F oven to dry out.

Preparation time: 10 minutes, plus 30 minutes draining time
Pressure cooking time: 20 minutes

Yield: 6 servings

⅔ cup canned pumpkin
5 slices day-old cinnamon-raisin bread

Unsalted butter, about 2 tablespoons
½ cup plus 2 tablespoons sugar
2 large eggs
4 large egg yolks
1 cup milk
1 tablespoon brandy or cognac
1 teaspoon pure vanilla extract
⅛ teaspoon salt
Freshly grated nutmeg to taste
2 cups water

1.   Line a strainer with paper toweling or cheesecloth. Add pumpkin and let drain at least 30 minutes. Butter a 6-cup pudding mold or baking dish that will fit easily inside the pressure cooker.

2.   Spread one side of each slice of bread with butter. Stack the slices and cut into cubes. Place them in the baking dish.

3.   Whisk the sugar, eggs, and egg yolks until light. Add milk, pumpkin, brandy, vanilla, salt, and nutmeg to taste and mix well. Pour over bread. Gently push the bread into the liquid to moisten it.

4.   Cover baking pan with aluminum foil so no water can get inside. Add 2 cups water to the pressure cooker. Put the baking dish in the steamer basket and place in the pressure cooker. Cover pressure cooker and bring up to full pressure (15 pounds). Reduce heat to stabilize pressure and cook for 20 minutes.

5.   Release pressure and remove steamer basket from pressure cooker. Carefully pour off any water that has accumulated on top of the foil, then remove foil. Serve warm or at room temperature. Bread pudding can be refrigerated for several days. Let stand at room temperature for about 15 minutes before serving.

OLD-FASHIONED BREAD PUDDING
WITH CARAMEL SAUCE

This is quite unlike most bread puddings in that it makes its own delicious sauce. When the cooked pudding is inverted, it is covered with a tawny gold crown of sweet caramel sauce. There is no sugar in the pudding itself—just in the sauce, so be sure each serving gets a generous helping of the sauce.

Preparation time: 10 minutes
Pressure cooking time: 25 minutes

Yield: 6 servings

4 slices day-old white bread
4 tablespoons unsalted butter
1 cup packed light brown sugar
1 tablespoon brandy
1½ cups half-and-half
2 large eggs
2 large egg yolks
1 teaspoon pure vanilla extract
Pinch salt
2 cups water

1.   Butter the bread with 2 tablespoons of the butter, then cut into cubes.

2.   Put the brown sugar in an even layer in the bottom of a 6-cup baking dish that fits comfortably inside the pressure cooker. Press any lumps from the sugar with the back of spoon. Cut the remaining 2 tablespoons butter into small pieces and dot over the sugar, then sprinkle with brandy. Add the cubed bread but do not stir.

3.   Whisk the half-and-half with the eggs, egg yolks, vanilla, and salt. Pour over the bread, again without stirring.

4.   Cover the baking dish with aluminum foil so that no water can get inside. Pour 2 cups water into the bottom of the pressure cooker. Place the baking dish in the steamer basket and add to pan. Cover pressure cooker and bring up to medium pressure (10 pounds). Reduce heat to stabilize pressure and cook for 25 minutes. Release pressure and remove baking dish. Pour off any water that has accumulated on top of foil, then remove foil.

5.   Run a knife around the edges of baking dish to loosen pudding from the sides. Invert a serving plate over the top of the baking dish and quickly turn the two pieces over. Remove the baking pan. Serve bread pudding warm or at room temperature.

INDEX